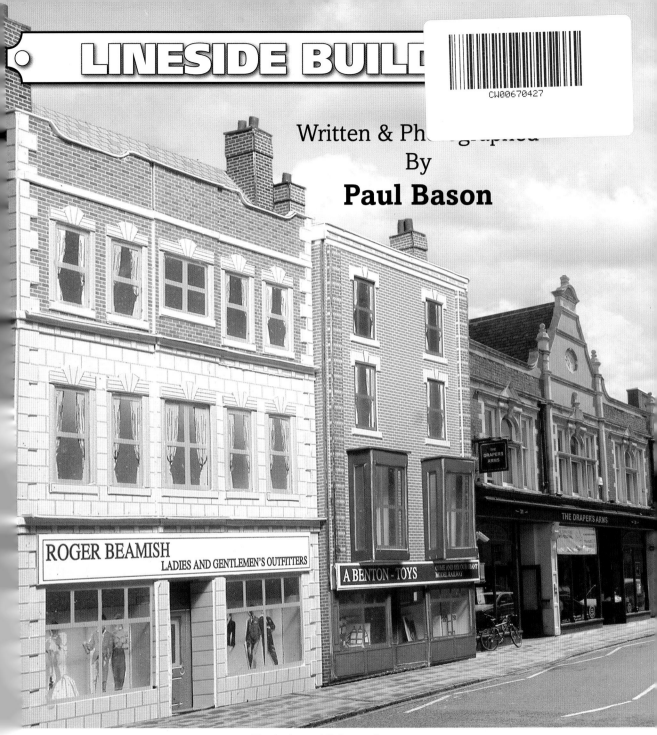

LINESIDE BUILD...

Written & Photographed
By
Paul Bason

CW00670427

From the publishers of
BRITISH RAILWAY MODELLING

Warners Group Publications Plc.,
The Maltings, West Street, Bourne, Lincolnshire PE10 9PH
Phone: 01778 391027 • Fax: 01778 425437

LINESIDE BUILDINGS

Have you ever admiringly reviewed some of the fantastic layouts regularly featured in the pages of *British Railway Modelling* and thought just how much you would like to emulate modellers like these but you just don't know where to start or perhaps simply don't feel that you have the skills to make a start? Well, in an attempt to inspire and inform both budding and exist enthusiasts alike, *Lineside Buildings* the first in a series of illustrated bo from the publishers of *British Rail Modelling* specially written to re

Paul Bason has over many years won acclaim for his scratch-building skills, having gained first place in many competitions for his 4mm scale cottages scratch-built from plastic card and for scratch-building EM gauge locomotives from brass as well. It is no surprise, therefore, that Paul's models, photographs and reviews have been a regular feature in the pages of British Railway Modelling since its very first issue over fifteen years ago. In real life Paul is a chartered quantity surveyor working for a large multi-national construction cost and management consultancy and is a keen railway photographer in his spare time.

t how easy the various facets of ut building can be.

Having chatted to many modellers ut making model buildings at shows r the years I am well aware that not model railway enthusiasts have the e, inclination, confidence or simply skills to scratchbuild structures like ones I enjoy making for my own ut. These modellers do however, still want good scale model buildings on their layouts but are often unsure of the best place to start. With these people in mind I hope to: -

- Introduce the newcomer to model railways to the various types of model buildings that are available in both ready-to-use and basic kit form
- Tempt those modellers who presently use ready to use buildings into having a go at true modelling with a simple plastic or card building kit
- Illustrate some of the more advanced types of kit on the market that are often perceived as too complicated by many modellers
- Offer an insight into some very basic and straightforward scratch-building techniques that might come in handy if you have a special building project in mind for the future.

Although we start with a quick look at a range of the tools, glues and adhesives needed to make up some of the kits described within these pages, the first buildings featured are from the land of ready made models where the layout builder has nothing more to do than to site the structure in place on the layout and build the scenery around it. Following this we then move on to review other ready-made models that need a few modelling skills such as painting to complete them, before taking a look at a whole host of model building kit types that are available to the railway modeller these days.

Between chapters you will find a variety of Prototype Inspiration pages to give you a few ideas of some of the building types that could add realism or interest to your layout. Here both real life and model photos come together to feature anything from signal boxes and stations to canals and corners shops.

Finally, having seen how etched building kits can be assembled without too much fuss, we see how straightforward scratch-building can be by making a plastic card base for the D&S etched LNER signal box superstructure kit.

In an attempt to encourage as many readers to get out their tools and have a go for themselves, I make no apology for including as many stage by stage photographs throughout the book as I can and, with a selection of scene suggestions created with the help of my computer's Photoshop package, I hope you will find something interesting and worthy of modelling for yourself.

Have Fun!

Paul Bason

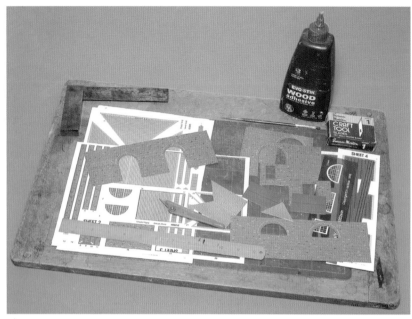

A small selection of basics tools and adhesives is all that you need to build card kits like this one.

If like me, you have been messing around constructing kits for years, you will, no doubt, already have a good selection of tools that will suit most modelling types and methods. If, on the other hand, you are new to the hobby or are just starting up again, it is probably worth taking a few moments to review some of the most useful tools, aids and adhesives that you will need to get started.

The following collection of tools will enable you to built up most basic kits: -
* Modelling knife with a good supply of new blades
* Steel rule or metal straight edge
* Razor saw
* A selection of small files
* Large flat and round files
* Propelling fibreglass brush
* Small pliers and cutters
* Small ordinary quality or old paint brushes for applying solvent
* Cutting mat (I use an A3 sized one)
* A pin vice

* A selection small drills
* A 4" engineer's square comes in very handy and is well worth the modest investment if you haven't already got one
* Task Lamp

If you want to make up an etched kit you will need to supplement the above with the following: -
* Soldering iron
* Soldering iron stand (not essential but most useful)
* Flux or soldering fluid
* Solder

Depending upon the type of kit, you might need the following to decorate or finish off your models: -
* Artists' crayons or felt tip pens (for colouring edges of card kits)
* Aerosol car primer (resin or metal kits)
* A selection of reasonable quality small paint brushes for painting
* A wide selection of coloured matt

enamels or acrylic paints
* Thinners for enamel paints
Finally, these glues and adhesives are worth keeping on the workbench: -
* PVA adhesive
* Liquid polystyrene cement
* Impact adhesive
* Quick setting epoxy resin
* Superglue
* Bostik UHU or similar

As you can see, the basic tools needed to set up your toolbox are really quite few and, for that matter, are relatively inexpensive to purchase. Indeed, it i very possible for your collection of such gadgets to be built up over a period o time as you become more proficient an adventurous in the models that yo build. Similarly, adhesives, which although it may be preferable to keep good supply of all types in the worksho in case they are needed, tend to m more specific to the type of kit and ca be bought in one at a time if you prefe

Having listed all of these useful iten it is probably work making menti that, although we as modellers u these glues and paints on a daily bas there are a number of quite serio heath and safety issues that aught to highlighted before we start work.

Firstly, always read the label of a glue, paint or solvent. Very often th have specific instructions regarding th safe use and in some cases tell you w to do if accidental misuse occurs. Ma products commonly advise you to them in a well-ventilated area example; if this is the case, simply k a window open and avoid breathing fumes. Some modern prod alternatives are much safer to use t their predecessors, Evo Stik in partic now make a solvent-free impact adhe which is just as good but a lot less sm than the old brown solvent-based var that some people still use. If you d

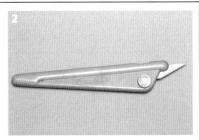

1. A cutting mat like this A3 sized one is a sound investment as is the steel rule seen on it. Note the strategically placed sheet of plastic card that hides my mat's very used and battle scarred appearance.

2. A typical inexpensive craft knife. I have been using this type of knife since I was at school! Always keep a good supply of new blades in stock as a blunt knife is of little use when cutting out card kits.

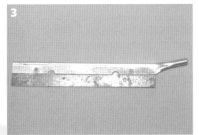

3. A razor saw can be used on most plastic, resin and metal kits.

4. An engineer's square is very handy for checking that the corners of buildings are at true right angles.

5. A selection of needle files is great for cleaning up plastic, resin and etched kits.

6. A few large files are an excellent way of smoothing off rough edges and fine-tuning joints as you put together plaster kits.

7. These two types of propelling fibre brush make light work of cleaning up brass or metal parts and can also be used to clean up the shiny surface of resin kits prior to painting.

8. A set of small drills and a pin vice will enable you to fit door handles and open up holes for rainwater pipes and the like.

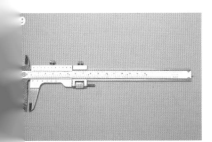

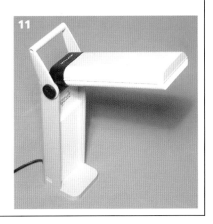

Vernier callipers are a nice to have tool for measuring inside and outside dimensions. They can also be used to ensure your models are fixed together squarely with nice, true parallel walls.

10. A selection of small pliers can be used for holding parts while etched parts are being soldered.

11. A modelling task light can be very useful. This one has a daylight simulating fluorescent fitting.

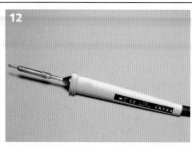

12. A soldering iron is a must for building etched kits. This one has a very useful variable heat control built in.
13. if you are going to buy a soldering iron, a stand like this will come in very handy too.

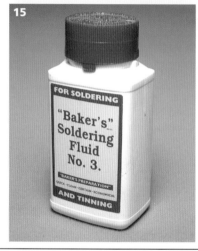

14. Multicore solder is just the lob for soldering etched kits together and is very useful when it comes to layout wiring too.
15. Baker's soldering fluid or a liquid flux helps solder run while soldering and tinning etched parts.

like the smell of enamel paint, why not try using acrylics instead?

Perhaps the most obvious safety tip is to be careful with your craft knife. Now I know I am not the world's safest user of these handy little tools, especially when I have just replaced the blade, but the odd cut finger can, if you are careful and watch what you are doing, really be avoided. Similarly, splashes and spray paint can be kept out of the model maker's eyes by a cheaply purchased pair of safety specs and you can also prevent the same stuff being breathed in by simply wearing a mask.

When it comes to children, it is pretty much common sense really; just keep those pretty coloured pots and jars either well out of reach or locked away from the little ones and always supervise the junior model maker when they are likely to be at risk.

Now that we are all 'tooled' up if you excuse the pun, and are ready to model in a safe environment, it is perhaps the best time to start our stroll through the various lanes of lineside buildings and kits available.

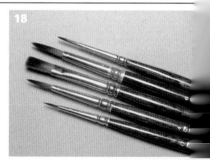

16. Artists' crayons are a simple way of colouring the exposed white edges around window openings and corners of printed card kits.

17. Aerosol car primer saves a lot of time and effort when preparing resin and etched kits for their final paint finish.

18. A selection of reasonable quality paint brushed will be needed for decorating all but the pre-coloured or printed model types.

19. Enamel paints have always been the modeller's favourite for both plastic and metal kits. Matt colours look better on buildings, if you can get them.
20. Acrylic paints can be used on both card, and plastic kits. A set like this is quite a cost-effective way to buy them.

21. Woodwork glue or white PVA adhesive is ideal for sticking together all types of paper and card kits.

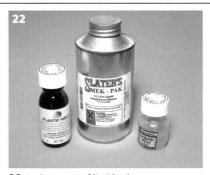

22. Various types of liquid polystyrene cement. Always remember to fully tighten the lid as it readily evaporates given half a chance.

23. Rather than use the old and smelly brown contact adhesive, this white solvent-free version is very useful for sticking plastic glazing to card, plastic metal or wood amongst other things.

24. Araldite Rapid is a fast drying epoxy resin adhesive well suited to gluing resin kits and most metals.

25. Various types and viscosities of superglue are available to the railway modeller. A medium thickness one is fine for general modelling.

27. Bostic adhesive is also used for card kits but can be stringy and messier than PVA.

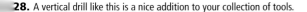

28. A vertical drill like this is a nice addition to your collection of tools.

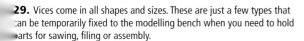

29. Vices come in all shapes and sizes. These are just a few types that can be temporarily fixed to the modelling bench when you need to hold parts for sawing, filing or assembly.

This delightful cottage is one of Harburn Hobbies Harburn Hamlet range of buildings.

As we start our review of the types of buildings available to the railway modeller, we find that there are several manufacturers who produce ready-made, ready-painted buildings and accessories that just need to be sited amongst the scenery. The majority of these models are made in 4mm and 2mm scales from a resin-bound plaster material although both plaster and plastic examples can also be found.

If you are the sort of model railway enthusiast that either doesn't feel that you have the skills needed to build kits or simply hasn't got the time to spend making and painting kits, these out-of-the-box buildings will, pardon the pun, be right up your street. Similarly, I also know

of layout builders who want a quick fix to their building problem and choose to temporarily populate their baseboards with buildings of this type while they are making real life prototypes up from scratch. Either way, the range of models open to you in 4mm and 2mm scales has broadened considerably in recent years with the advent of the Harburn Hobbies, and more recently Hornby collections.

Such is the popularity of these buildings that many collectors, not just of the model railway fraternity, now buy these structures to keep on their shelves. A couple of Hornby's earlier examples are in fact featured here for comparison with their more recent offerings. I think that the newer releases are in general much

better but are not quite perfect, still falli into the trap of using the wrong bri bond pretty much throughout the rang

As there is no stage-by-sta construction process to show you, few pointers may help you select a position buildings, generally whetl ready-made or otherwise.

Firstly, when you are planning yo layout or diorama, it is well worth draw up a scale plan of the baseboard show exactly the space you have available lineside buildings and scenery genera This will then allow you to be able roughly pencil in your thoughts for buildings that you need to bring the lay to life. Before you start spending mo: why not have a look through the var

This unusual water mill was one of Hornby's first Skaledale models back in 2003.

Poacher's Cottage was another early example of a Skaledale structure that has now become a collector's item.

...anufacturers catalogues to check ...ailability (I find that websites are best). ...so, wherever possible, find out the plan ...es of the models that you are interested It is at this stage that you often find

that buildings are a little larger than you at first imagine, so be ready to fine-tune your pencil plan in case. If you plan is large enough, or better still full-size, try cutting out rectangles of card that can act

as movable templates and help you locate everything before you begin. As your design takes shape, try to group buildings together in a realistic way, I often find that scenes have a better visual appearance if they are things out at an angle to the railway or the baseboard edge. Have a look at some of the layouts featured in British Railway Modelling for ideas and inspiration and you will see just what I mean.

Now that we have looked at layout design and placement, we can pictorially review some of the structures available from the leading contenders starting with Harburn Hobbies in 4mm scale, Hornby's Skaledale range (also in 4mm) and finally Lyddle End, Hornby's 2mm scale series.

Hornby's Liddle End collection of buildings are for the 2mm scale N gauge modeller. They include a host of terraced houses pictured here

Harburn Hobbies Buildings

This brick-built workman's bothy is ideal for yards and industrial settings.

Above: This country garage is enhanced by some of the cast accessories al available from Harburn Hobbies.

A complimentary admin' office is also available.

Just some of the scenic odds and ends that Harburn Hobbies manufacture.

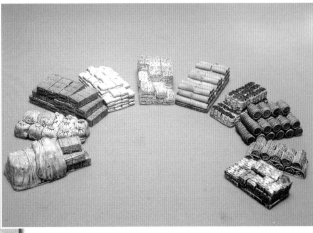

An assortment of loads such as these can quickly add interest to both wagons and the lineside.

A farm shop like this makes an interesting addition to the rural diorama.

Post boxes, too, are available from Harburn Hobbies.

Phone boxes are very useful for the roadside.

Harburn Hobbies make these rustic fishermen's worksheds together with all of the nets, creels and general junk that you need to go with them.

The admin' office makes an excellent coal office for the station yard.

Keep left signs and a flower-covered traffic island for the urban scene.

...lection of Harburn's street and park furniture.

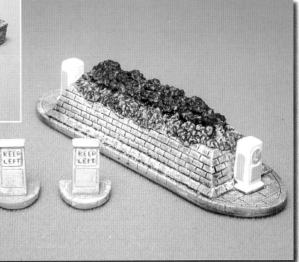

Holy Trinity church is an imposing structure for those layouts with plenty of spare space.

A scene made using Skaledale's terraced houses and shop.

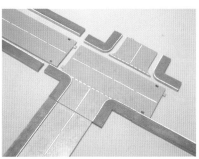

These modular roads and pavements make road building a piece of cake.

Hornby also supply a selection of bridges like this one.

The underside of a typical Skaledale model - note the hole to permit lighting.

Hornby's Skaledale range of terraced houses and shops can make a
splendid mix and match urban scene.

The Saracen's Head pub i
well suited to any town c
country settin

If you want to be much more adventurous the Skaledale gas works will make an interesting way to fill the lineside.

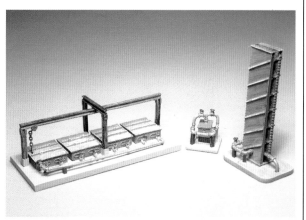

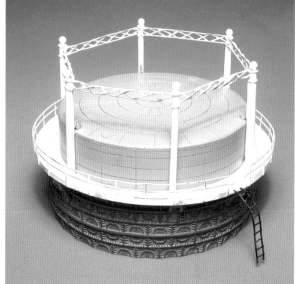

nby also produce a range of pre-painted figures to compliment their dings.

Accessory packs like these are handy additions to the scenery.

Hornby Hobbies Lyddle End Buildings

This quaint oasthouse and farm building are ideal for a Kentish farm scene

St Andrew's church.

This collection of 2mm scale buildings make construction of a complete station scene very simple.

...se tiny shops can be used to make a village street scene.

The completed row of industrial buildings.

Taking a step up the modelling ladder, we come across several types of model building that can be purchased in a pretty much complete but totally unpainted form. As with the ready-made buildings that we have just seen, the layout builder often has a choice of either low relief or complete buildings.

Falling into this category we find such niceties as the 2mm scale/N gauge low relief factory and office modules from Ten Commandments and the wide range of basic low relief buildings in 4mm scale/00 gauge manufactured by Townstreet. Both ranges are cast in a very fine plaster-based material which, with the exception of a small amount of cleaning up, only needs painting to be ready to place on the layout.

In an attempt to inspire readers who don't actively model at the moment to have a go for themselves, we will take a quick look at the stages needed to prepare a row of simple industrial buildings for the layout.

Ten Commandments Factory Units

This handy range of 2mm scale industrial building facades is ideal for hiding those awkward and often untid[y] joints where the baseboard meets th[e] backscene. If used carefully, low reli[ef] castings such as these will not only a[...]

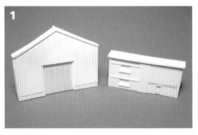

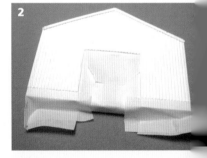

1. The low relief castings as they come.
2. The wall is masked off ready for spraying.

3. The whole lot is given a coat of grey car primer.

4. The tape is removes revealing the areas [to] be hand-painted.

more interest to the diorama but can also give an added impression of depth to the layout.

Supplied as individual modular units, you can buy as few or as many factory and office section sections as you want and for that matter, arrange them in any order whatsoever. As they come, the plaster castings don't really need any work to them at all. I think I literally had to give the edges a quick rub around with a small file but that was all.

Being already white painting is really very easy to do. If you wish you can paint each factory section different colours. As however, one of the most common colours of wall cladding and roof sheeting in the building industry is 'Goosewing Grey' you can, like me, adopt this shade and save a little time in the process. The trick up my sleeve is to spray the cladding with ordinary grey car primer bought ready to use in an aerosol from my local car parts shop. As we don't want to cover up the white plaster finish where the other colours are to be applied, it is best to mask these off first. The easiest way of doing these is to take a strip of masking tape and temporarily stick it to a flat surface such as a cutting mat or something similar. Then, using a sharp knife, cut off small strips that can be stuck piece by piece over the areas to be unpainted until the whole model is masked. If you wish you can try to accurately mark and cut out whole areas at a time but from experience I can assure you that it is far quicker and easier to stick strips of masking tape on in easy stages. Make sure that you have pressed the tape down firmly to ensure that you have a good seal and you are ready to spray.

When spraying paint of any kind always remember to:-
- Make sure the room is well ventilated· Cover up and protect all surrounding surfaces
- Wear a face mask and protective glasses
- using an aerosol, shake the can well

- Spray the paint evenly
- Apply several thin coats rather than one thick one that is liable to run
- Leave the paint to dry thoroughly before recoating or moving on to the next stage

With the cladding now painted grey, it is time to pick out the detailing. To do this I prefer to use matt enamels from the Humbrol range but acrylic paints, if you have them, should do the job equally as well. Now all you have left to do is to mount the models at the edge of the baseboard and the job is done!

Ten Commandments LNER Huts

Again manufactured in plaster, these two versions of the LNER platelayers hut are very easy to use. The 7mm version is a little more complicated and will be seen a bit later in this book.

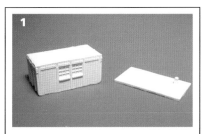

1.The 4mm hut is supplied in two parts that need to be glued together using pva glue.

2. The 4mm hut is ready to paint in no time at all.

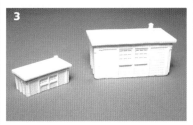

3. The 2mm hut comes in one piece and makes an interesting comparison with its 4mm stalemate.

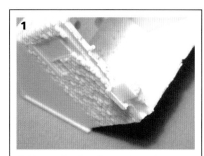

1. The rough edge of the resin casting

2. The edge is trimmed using a razor saw.

3. Two buildings prepared and ready to paint.

Gramodels Resin Buildings

As an alternative to plaster, some manufacturers prefer to make their buildings from resin. One such firm, Gramodels, produces a small number of buildings mainly in 2mm scale to accompany their extensive range of military accessories. One particularly useful model, a corrugated Nissen hut, is manufactured in resin for modellers in 2mm, 4mm and even 7mm scales.

In the accompanying photos you will see that some preparation work on these resin models ready for painting is needed, namely that you just have to trim off the bottom edge of the casting with a razor saw and tidy up the cut line with a small file.

Fitzgerald's Bar.

N estling alongside the line from Dublin to Wexford is the picturesque village of Avoca in County Wicklow in Ireland. Made famous as a filming location some years ago by the hit BBC drama Ballykissangel. Avoca, and its focus, Fitzgerald's Bar, have since become a magnet for tourists. It is not surprising, therefore, that a model based on the pub has been produced in low-relief form by Birmingham-based Alphagraphix. The kit itself is very easy and straightforward to make, although you do have to cut out all of the parts, and comes in a form that you could alternatively build as a complementary pair of cottages.

Avoca is better known as the setting for the BBC drama Ballykissangel.

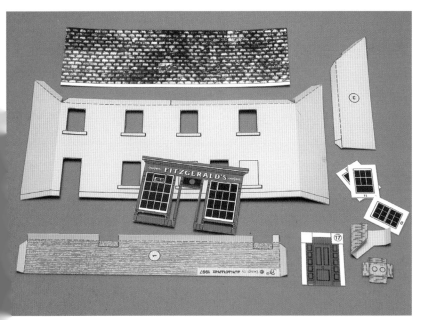

The kit is cut out ready for assembly.

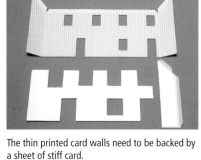

The thin printed card walls need to be backed by a sheet of stiff card.

Windows and window surrounds are added as construction progresses.

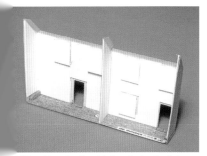

Additional bracing is added to the back of the model.

Window sills and wall details are fixed next.

The model is transformed by the addition of the bar's frontage.

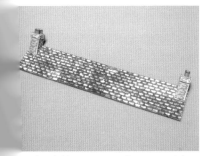

roof and chimneys are made up separately.

completed pub – now, where's my pint of black stuff?

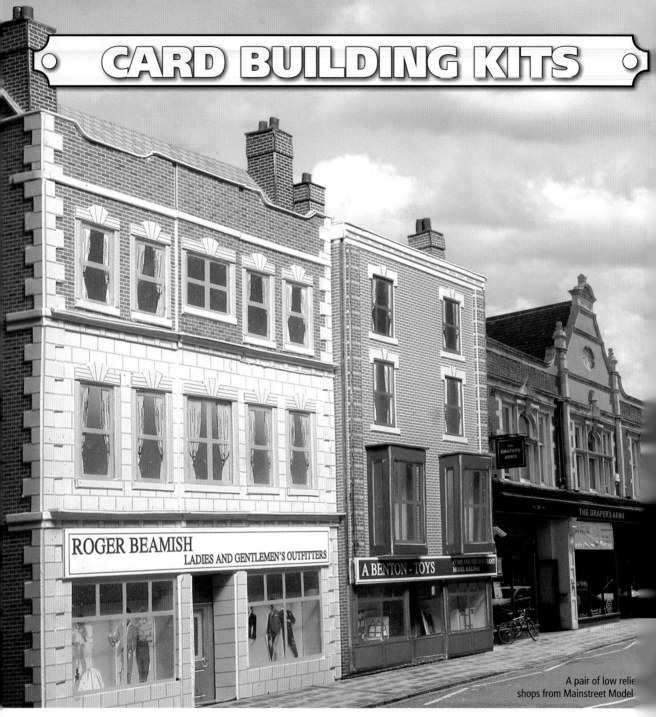

A pair of low relie
shops from Mainstreet Model

Card kits have, over the years, given many model makers an easy introduction into the ways of true kit building and as a result have been the catalyst that sets the enthusiast on the right track to grander things. I certainly remember messing about with Superquick kits as a small boy, as I am sure do a good many others.

The present day card building kit market is very buoyant with a wide range of kits being available in scales from 2mm to 7mm. If you want to know just what is available a good place to look is in Freestone Model Accessories' mail order catalogue or on their extensive stand at shows. Proprietor Jerry Freestone takes pride in stocking almost everything

available in card and also r manufactures the Prototype Mod Howard Scenics, Mainstreet Mod Bilteezi and Modelyard ranges of kits

Pretty much irrespective of the m of card kit that you purchase the b assembly process involves: -
• Familiarisation with the parts instructions

- Removal of the individual pieces/cutting out
- Scribing and folding
- Strengthening or backing
- Colouring cut card edges
- Making and fitting of the windows and doors
- Final assembly

This said, the fine detail of the process does vary a little from make to make, so with this in mind, we will take a closer look at a representative selection of some common types of card kits that are available. Before we do so it is, however, well worth considering some of the tips of the trade common to them all.

Cutting Out

Top of my tip list has got to be cutting. Whether the card kit comes pre-cut or not you will still need to have a sharp craft knife and some spare blades ready for action. To go with this, a decent sized cutting mat and a 12" long steel rule are ideal.

Now I know many modellers buy pre-cut kits to save all of the hassle involved with the cutting out process, but from experience, I find it well worth the time spent cutting through the tiny card 'pips' that hold these kits together in the packet. OK, so even I am often tempted to push out the parts in a fit of eagerness, but if you do you can readily rip the surface of the card and end up with an untidy edge that will still need

trimming with a knife anyway.

Where card parts have to be cut out from the offset, it is always best to do so using a new knife blade and, wherever possible, using the steel rule as a guide. A cutting mat, although not truly essential, does make an excellent base for the task in hand, particularly as it has no grain like a sheet of plywood that can easily make your nice straight line veer off course.

When cutting out windows, I always remove the centre of the aperture first such that a few millimetres is left on the waste side of the true aperture line. This makes the removal of the last thin strip very easy as it has less resistance from the card to cut against. To keep things looking neat and crisp always remember to cut away from the corners of an aperture and you won't go far wrong.

Scoring and Folding

Most kits involve some form of folding to shape around score lines. Although some do come pre-scored, most card kits involve the modeller having to partly cut through or score the card's surface. This is best done by lightly running the craft knife along the fold line using the rule as a guide and making sure that not too much pressure is applied such that the part is cut right through. The general principle is that the score needs to be on the outside face of the printed part to allow the card to be folded back (such as a corner) but,

where there is a reverse angle, the back of the part may need to be scribed instead. In this case, simply make small cuts through the card at the two ends of the fold line as seen from the front, turn the sheet over and score between the two cut marks and the fold is ready to form

Glueing

When making up kits of this type I prefer to use two types of glue. The first is white PVA woodwork adhesive and the second is a solvent-free contact adhesive such as the Evo-stik product illustrated earlier.

As you can probably guess, I use the PVA for all card to card joints but prefer to employ the contact adhesive for the fitting of plastic glazing, curtains and the like. Similarly, the latter comes in handy if you have any metal (like whitemetal chimneys) to fix in place. Both being water-based they can, in theory, if applied too thickly, affect the paper or card causing it to warp. In practice, however, I, having built up a whole load of kits for this book, haven't experienced any adverse effects at all.

If you prefer, and as recommended by some manufacturers, you can fix your kits together with a general purpose glue such as UHU or Bostic. This has the advantage of being usable throughout the whole process but can, if not used very carefully, leave messy strings of glue just where you don't want on the printed surface.

Selection of kits available from Freestone Model Accessories.

This 7mm scale signal box is by Alphagraphix.

Superquick Country Church

When I was at school in the late 1970s and had a Saturday job at the late John Fowler's Peterborough Model Shop, Superquick's excellent series of pre-cut and pre-scored card kits were undoubtedly the market leaders in their field. Since then, despite the appearance of some 'new kids on the block', Superquick kits still remain very popular with the model railway fraternity and are ideal candidates for inclusion in this publication.

If you look carefully at the country church kit you will see that it is actually printed on thin card that is already backed for you with thicker card. With all of the main parts pre-cut all you have to do is to simply run the tip of a craft knife blade around the edge of each part to release them from the sheet. With clear red marker arrows printed on waste areas of card to identify the fold lines, the bending of corners and fixing tabs is really easy to

follow. It would be misleading to say that the whole kit is cut out for you as, in reality, a small number of parts on the thinner printed card part of the sheet actually have to be cut to size, scored and folded to shape. Just use a sharp knife and a straight edge and you will have no problems with this at all.

The photographic sequence clearly illustrates just how straightforward

assembly really is, provided, of cours that you stick to the instructions, glue a fold all of the tabs as directed and fix t corners strengtheners provided in plac The only awkward, or more accurate fiddly bit is the folding and forming of t church's spire and its unusual shap base. If you take your time even this soon completed and is ready to cap yet another interesting little model.

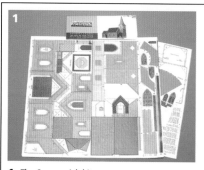

1. The Superquick kit.

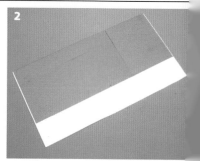

2. The reverse side of the pre-thickened card k

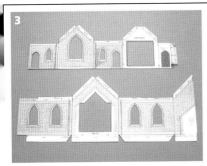

3. The walls are removed from the sheet.

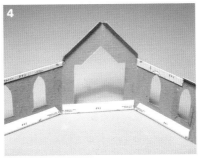

4. Tabs are folded over and glued.

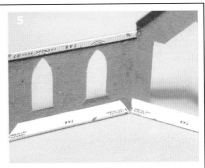

5. Note the instructions printed on the tabs.

6. Assembly starts with the tower.

7. Corners are reinforced with card strengtheners.

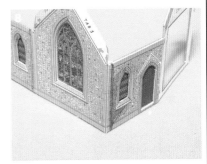

8. Stained glass windows are fixed prior to assembly.

9. The tower and chancel are glued together.

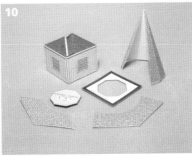

10. Various parts make up the belfry and spire.

11. The porch parts are made up ready to fit to the main assembly.

12. The nave and porch walls are added next.

13. Roof sections are added to the assembly.

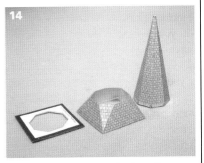

14. The spire sections are glued together.

Metcalfe's Coaching Inn.

Metcalfe Models Card Kits

In more recent years, card kit manufacturer, Metcalfe Models have really, pardon the pun, gone to town with an extensive and exciting collection of building kits for both 4mm and 2mm scales. Being pre-cut and pre-scored, these kits are really easy to put together and are well suited to the modelling capabilities of most modellers.

Metcalfe's kits have a couple of outstanding features that are well worth a mention. Firstly, the fixing tabs and waste card in many of their kits are commendably annotated with written details that clearly show the builder exactly what goes where and just how the whole thing fixes together.

The second is that Metca[...] instructions are, I feel, probably the [...] presented of any card kit range on [...] market. Not only do they lead the m[...] maker through the construction pro[...] in a simple easy to follow stage-by-s[...] manner, but they also feature a whole [...] of clear well-drawn three-dimensi[...] sketches that highlight all of the are[...]

Coaching Inn

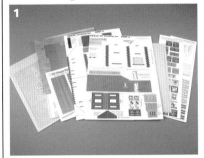

1. The pre-cut printed card kit.

2. The two wings are made up separately before being stuck together.

3. The completed inn from behind.

Bus Garage

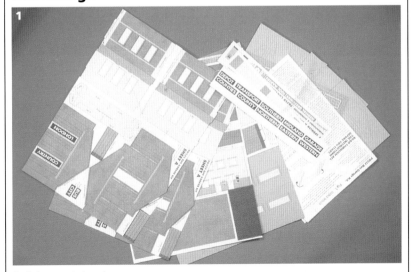

1. Before we start work.

rest and possible concern.

Having delved deep into the *British* ?*way Modelling* archives, I have found ?lection of photos that I have taken of ?calfe's kits to illustrate product reviews ?r the years. I hope these images ably ?trate just a few of Metcalfe's methods ?construction and reveal just how ?ghtforward assembly can be.

Bus Garage Cont

2. The main folding doors are fitted before assembly.

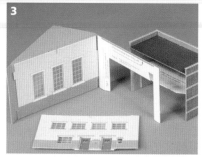

3. Assembly begins with the offices and one end of the building.

4. The roof structure.

5. The completed bus garage.

6. The rear of the garage could be used as an industrial unit.

Church

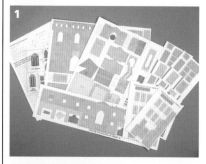

1. Another load of parts.

2. Construction commences with the tower.

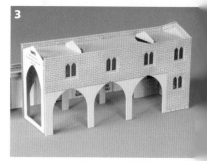

3. The main structure during assembly.

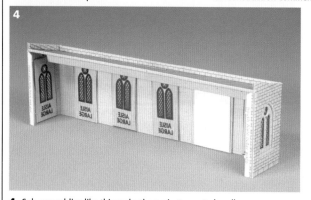

4. Sub-assemblies like this make the project easy to handle.

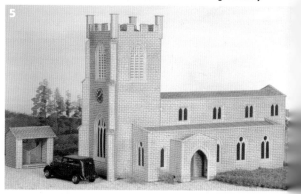

5. The completed church.

Engine Shed

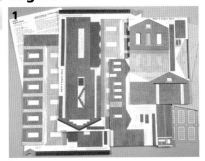

1. Even more printed card bits.

2. The construction notes can clearly be seen at this stage of construction.

3. The engine shed is finished and awaits locating on the layout.

Brewery

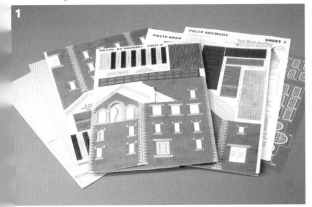

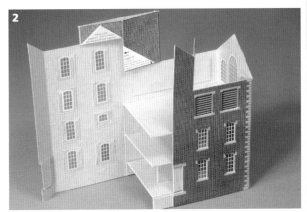

1. Yet more card parts.

2. The part-assembled kit.

Ready for business – I hope they brew real ale!

The completed Modelyard goods shed in action.

Modelyard Goods Shed

Another popular range of pre-cut out card kits is the series of lineside buildings manufactured by Modelyard. Unlike those from Superquick and Metcalfe, these do not rely on tabs and folds to generally hold the corners and parts together but instead employ the use of square wooden section blocks which not only join the pieces but also reinforce the joints at the same time.

As illustrated by the photos, you will see that the strip of wood provided has to be cut to length before being stuck to one side of the joint using woodwork/ PVA glue. When this has been given sufficient time to dry, the adjoining part

can then be simply glued to it, ensuring as you do, that all is square and true. I will admit that I have used more wood strips to reinforce the goods shed than you get in the kit, largely as it stiffens the structure and prevents the long walls from twisting out of shape. I bought a long length of slightly larger section square timber from B&Q for a couple of pounds some time ago so that I had some to come in handy at times like these- isn't it a good job that I did?

Modelyard buildings do have another departure from the card kit norm. In an attempt to prevent the inside being too visible, Modelyard provide pre-printed clear plastic glazing with a dark smoked

finish. As you can see this does look little unusual when you are building the model but really looks quite go when it is finished and placed in a railw setting.

Perhaps the only other thing worthy a special mention with kits from t manufacturer is that the tab-less r structure does need to be taped toget to hold it in alignment while you glue joints between the slopes together. At f I remember finding this a little awkw to do without the whole thing mov about but, after a bit of trial and error, some strategically placed tape, s became used to the method and in end completed the roof in no time at a

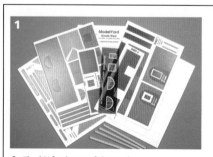

1. The kit fresh out of the packet.

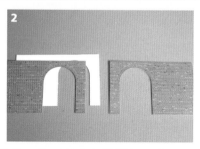

2. The walls are backed with thicker card.

3. An artist's crayon or felt tipped pen is idea for colouring the cut edges.

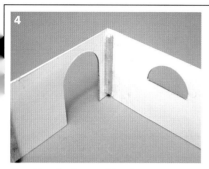

4. Unlike other kits, Modelyard use square section timber to hold things together.

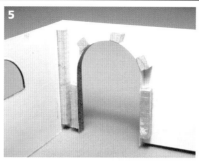

5. Pieces of wood also hold the brick arch linings in place.

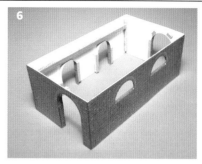

6. As assembly progresses, additional strips of timber can strengthen the structure

7. The printed plastic windows are stuck in place.

8. The goods office is made up and attached to the main building.

9. The internal platform is assembled in isolation.

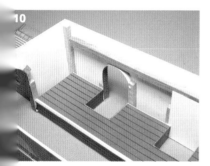

10. It is then fixed in place inside the goods shed.

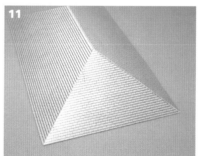

11. The roof is folded up into shape.

12. Clear tape can temporarily hold the slopes in place as the glue sets.

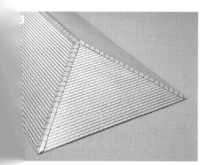

Ridges and hips are stuck over the joints.

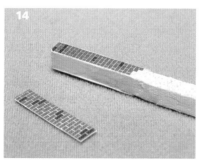

14. The chimney also uses a length of timber for its core.

15. The goods shed ready for use.

The completed Antiques Shop and Café.

Bilteezi Kits

Originally produced by Hamblings of Charing Cross, the large range of inexpensive Bilteezi whole and low-relief building sheets has been popular with railway modellers for many decades. Although they are not as complicated or have quite the level of raised detailing or relief as some of the more recent card kits, these sheets certainly make up into some of the most interesting prototypes on the model railway market.

As you can see there are no windows to cut out (unless of course you want to replace them with clear glazed ones) and the amount of work needed to build them up certainly reflects their 'built easy' tag. Generally, all you, the modeller, have to do is to cut out the parts, fold them up to shape and finally glue them all together. Having said this, there is a slight complication. Due largely to the thin card (or is it thick paper?) that these buildings are printed on, I really feel that some kind of strengthening is required.

To give the completed model both strength and rigidity it is best to measure, mark out and cut backing pieces of stiff (at least 1mm thick) card that can be glued behind all of the main walls and roof slopes. Similarly, false floors can be made from the same material using the templates provided. As a word of warning, just be a little careful whilst making these strengtheners; don't forget to ensure that you compensate for their thickness at corners. If you wish to super-reinforce the joints, why not add little blocks of 5mm x 5mm timber strip just as Modelyard do with their kits?

With excellent artwork and optional parts often included, these building sheets are ideal as a base for kit-bashing and improving. I have already suggested that the windows could be replace with glazing such as Downesglaze, and a host of other improvements are relatively easy to do. In this instance the flat sheet of the timber-framed row of shops could easily be given some

additional relief. For another couple quid you could buy a second sheet t▮ would enable you to cut out and mo▮ the timber framing which can then stuck over the printed framing givin▮ a realistic raised appearance. Simila▮ the doors could be set back a little ▮ a couple of kits fixed together c▮ give you a longer row of shops ▮ houses; the options with a l▮ imagination really are endless.

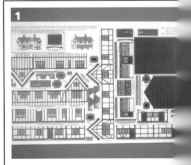

1. The whole kit is printed on a single sh▮ of thin card.

2. Parts are easily cut out using a sharp knife and straight edge.

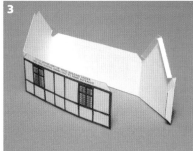

3. The parts are too flexible to be left unstrengthened.

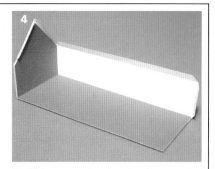

4. Thicker mounted card needs to be cut to size and fitted inside the model.

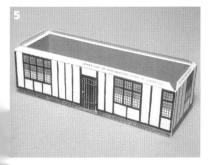

5. The lower walls are folded and are held together by glued tabs.

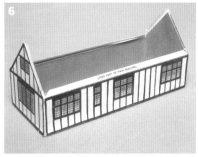

6. The upper walls are similarly treated.

7. The upper and lower sections are then stuck on top of each other.

The various wings are made up as sub-semblies.

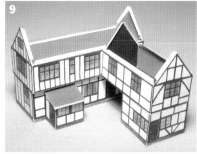

9. The various parts are then stuck together.

10. Stiffening pieces are also added to the undersides of the roof slopes.

. All of the roof sections are glued on top of walls.

12. The half-timbered house just needs chimneys to complete.

13. Simple card overlays convert the house into a pair of shops.

Many kits take their inspiration from actual prototype buildings and Modelyard's red brick station building is no exception. It is in fact based upon the ex Great Northern Railway station buildings at Welwyn North close to the famous viaduct on the East Coast Main Line. As you can see from the photographic comparison, the design has been simplified to make reproduction in card possible, but the overall model is quite pleasing and is well worth a second look.

Welwyn North as seen today from the station approach.

Another view from the car park.

The platform side of the building.

Welwyn North's Up platform.

e completed Modelyard building.

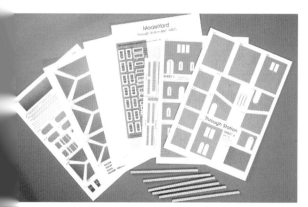

elyard's Welwyn North kit.

The various sub-assemblies are made in isolation.

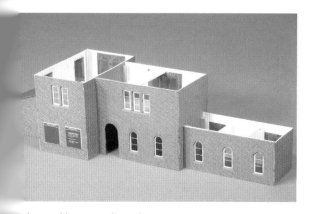

b-assemblies are stuck together.

The roof is added one stage at a time.

Further embellishments are added to the front elevation.

Mainstreet Shops

Out of all of the varieties of card kits that I have built up during the making of this book, Mainstreet's collection of low-relief shops are some of the most time consuming. This isn't because they are particularly difficult to put together but just because they require the builder to carefully cut out every individual part and have a lot of windows to make up.

Looking through the illustrations you will see that, having cut out the main walls, each of the windows is fixed in place in turn (together with printed paper curtains) before assembly proper can get underway. To strengthen the printed sheets, you are supplied with a sheet of mounting board to make backing pieces and false floors. Luckily, in this instance, you don't have to mark these out for yourself. Mainstreet thoughtfully provide paper templates that can be stuck to the thicker card and cut around to do the job for you.

In common with other card kits, you do need to take a little time to colour in the cut edges of the card parts prior to sticking them together. This simple exercise greatly improves the finish of the model and avoids any unsightly strips of white card showing through. I find this best done using artists' crayons or felt-tipped pens.

Otherwise assembly is pretty much as any other card kits, although you do have to carefully add the decorative brick and stonework detailing so commonly found on town centre buildings of this type as the structure takes shape. Finally, to cap it all off there is a simple-to-make card roof and some easily-built chimney stacks.

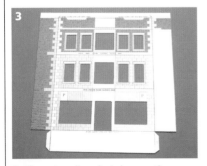

5. Printed glazing is cut out and contact adhesive is applied.

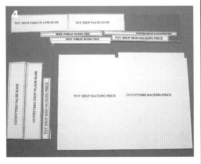

6. Each window is individually glazed.

7. The glazing in place.

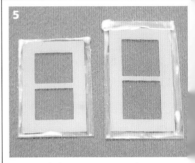

1. The printed card sheets.

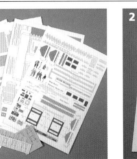

2. The centres of the windows are removed prior to cutting proper.

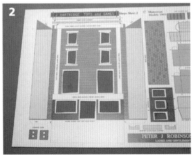

3. The main walls and windows are then neatly cut out.

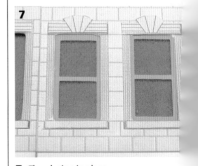

4. Templates are provided for making stiffening pieces.

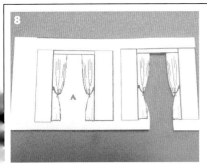

8. Paper curtains are supplied in the kit.

9. The curtains are fixed behind the glazing.

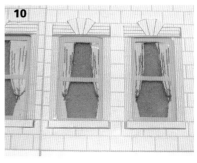

10. The completed window.

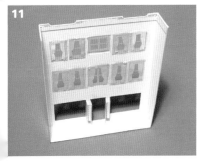

11. The outfitters during its first stage of assembly.

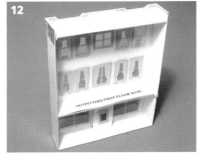

12. False floors stiffen the model.

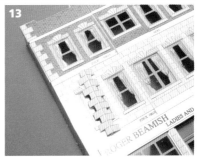

13. Additional card layers add stone detail.

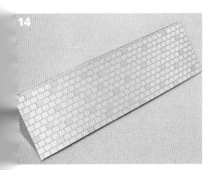

4. The roof is made up separately.

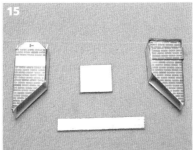

15. Typical card chimneys.

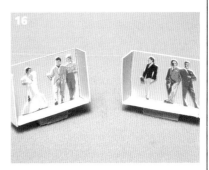

16. Window interiors are provided in the kit.

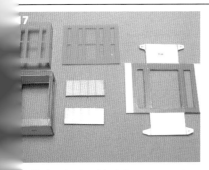

7. The toy shop's oriel window components.

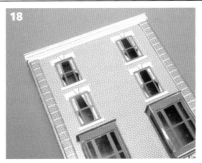

18. The windows are assembled and fitted.

19. Almost complete – just the chimneys and window displays to add.

Howard Scenics Terrace

Although there are only a few models in the Howard Scenics range, their quality is really pretty good. Obviously aimed at the more experienced builder, they feature a number of differences from most card kits.

The first, and most noticeable is that the facing sheets are printed on paper rather than card and that all walls are thickened using mounting board. I understand that the idea behind this is so that you don't actually have to score the corners in able to fold them. Having tried this I personally find that the resulting corner is not quite as crisp as a scored one and have lightly scored the fold lines in this instance to ensure they are in the desired place. Luckily paper templates are provided to assist you in cutting out the backing sheets to

size. These need to be lightly covered with glue and laminated to the paper walls, and also made up into strengthening pieces to provide additional support.

Another feature is that the paper sheet is cut and folded through the apertures in the backing sheet to line the sides, or reveals, of the windows and doors. The waste paper tab is then used to secure the lining on the back of the wall.

To make up the sash windows Howard Scenics provide two layers of pre-printed clear plastic glazing. Once cut out, these have to be stuck together before being fixed into position on the walls. No problems here but they really are a vast improvement on the etched ones that this manufacturer used to supply when the kits came out some years ago.

Even the roof is different from the

card kit norm. Here we find individu strips of slates that have to be cut o and stuck onto the plain card base overlapping rows. The whole thing crowned by whitemetal chimney p that yet again are a departure from t norm of card kit construction.

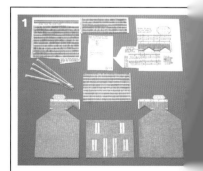

1. The first job is to cut out the parts.

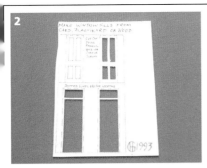

2. Doors and frames comprise several layers of card.

3. The thin walls are bonded to a backing layer of thick card.

4. Note how the printed walls wrap around the sides of the window and door apertures.

5. The chimney stack is folded up ready to be filled with scraps of thick card.

6. The doors are fixed in place.

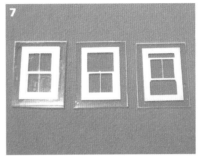

7. Windows are made from two layers of printed glazing.

These are then added to the walls.

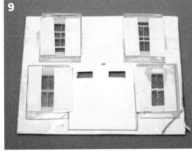

9. Paper curtains can be glued in place behind the glazing.

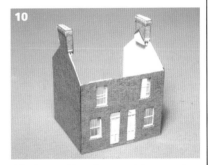

10. The two side walls are stuck in turn to the front elevation.

A card roof is added next.

12. Strips of overlapping slates make a realistic roof covering.

13. The roof is covered.

With the main building, a platform shelter, level crossing and signal box, Heckington is a very model worthy subject.

Heckington on Lincolnshire's Grantham to Boston cross-country route is famed for two main things. Firstly, it is home to a rare eight-sailed windmill, which incidentally dominates the southern side of the station scene, and secondly, it is the inspiration for the Prototype Models station building kit. As you can see from the photographic comparison, this sizeable structure, as the manufacturer's name suggests, is a pretty accurate representation of its ex-Great Northern Railway prototype. Heckington's modelling potential is

The prototype kit's inspiration seen from the level crossing

much boosted by the survival of brick-built goods shed, timber platf[...] shelter, impressive signal box, sig[...] and level crossing. If you really adventurous and have room, why include the windmill as well?

Heckington's station approach

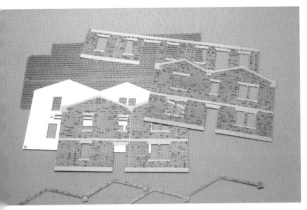

The kit is cut out ready for assembly.

Sash windows are added to the walls.

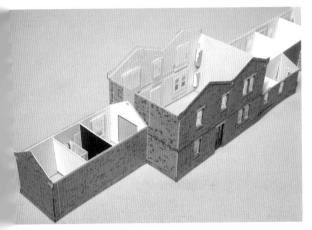

Assembly is well under way with additional strengthening being added as required.

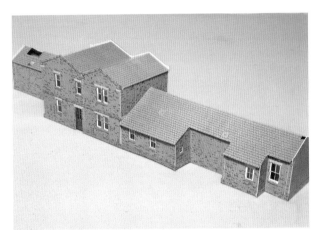

With the roof in place, just the chimneys and downpipes need to be added.

...ington station seen from the platform side.

This impressive Great Western footbridge was built by Michael Warner using Hornby kits.

When it comes to model building construction kits, plastic, or rather injection-moulded polystyrene kits have always been a pretty popular choice with the model railway fraternity. Being on the whole, easy to assemble, such kits offer the layout builder a relatively quick and straightforward way of adding lineside interest to the scene. Unlike ready to fix models, they are in fact, each an individual modelling project and often give the modeller his first taste of any form of kit building. With kits available to suit most scales and gauges from Z to

G, models of this type are well worth reviewing in detail.

Manufacturers like Dapol, Ratio, Hornby and Peco have over the years served the hobby well with numerous British-outline lineside kits, as have smaller but less well known concerns such as Dornoplas and Kestrel Designs. Many American, and European kits from big names such as Faller, Pola and Heljan also proved popular, particularly where they are not too continental in appearance. As a medium, polystyrene is great to work with and easily enables standard as-bought kits to be modified,

combined or generally kit-bash without too much fuss at all. Inde some of the quaint structures from other side of the North Sea can, in fa be easily Anglicised to suit the Brit scene despite their HO scale of 3.5m to 1 foot being marginally smaller th the 4mm to 1 foot scale adopted by C

Plastic kits tend to fall into following main categories:-
• Unpainted kits
• Pre-coloured kits
• Pre-coloured kits with self-adhe printed paper overlays
• Wills Craftsman range of kits

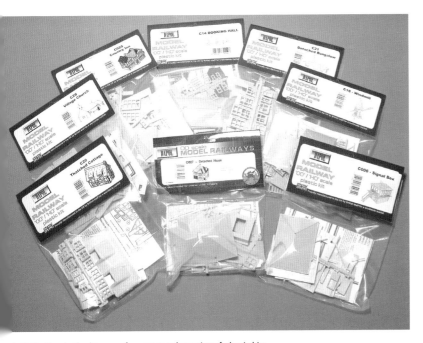

is Ratio Goods Shed is one of a very popular series of plastic kits.

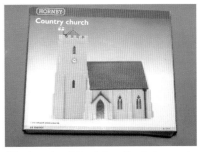

This discontinued church from Hornby is a good example of a pre-coloured kit.

An example of the Wills Craftsman range of model buildings.

Each type of kit has advantages and sadvantages. Obviously some of ese will be subjective - the need for inting the completed model for ample might fall into both categories pending whether you like painting or t. Pre-coloured kits can indeed save ot of modelling time but can in some tances look a bit too 'glossy' and lly do benefit from a coat of paint. practice you often find that, despite ur best endeavours, any glue or vent that strays onto the plastic face during construction fades and rks the surface to some extent. hough the obvious answer is to be y careful when you are applying the e, it is often just as well to remedy situation and paint the coloured tic anyway. Needing much more delling experience than most other tic buildings, Wills Craftsman kits ally contain sheets of their ossed stonework, brickwork and ing that have to be marked and cut using templates provided. Bordering scratchbuilding with instructions, do contain moulded windows and gs.

With the exception of the latter, which will be treated in isolation, the same basic construction processes have to be followed whatever the type or scale of kit that you want to build, these are: -

- Study the instructions
- Remove parts from the sprue
- Familiarise yourself with the kit
- Clean up any flash
- Stick the parts together
- Paint as required.

Plastic kits of European or American prototypes like this one on Bob Tidball's Arcadia layout often need little modification for the British Scene.

Dapol's thatched cottage kit in a country setting.

Dapol Thatched Cottage

As an introduction to constructing plastic kits, it is probably worth looking at a few examples that vary both in complexity and design. A good starting point for our review is the simple-to-make 4mm scale thatched cottage from Dapol.

In common with all plastic kits, the first task is to remove the parts from the sprues that hold them together in transit and act as a means of feeding the plastic material into the moulds during the injection moulding process. Now I know that the easiest and perhaps most tempting way to remove parts is to simply

pull or twist them away from the sprue, and in most cases you will be able to do this reasonably successfully. The problem is if the release is not clean and some plastic from the part breaks away with the sprue leaving an unsightly gap in the piece that will inevitably be difficult to hide or fill in.

To prevent this from occurring, the best way is to cut the parts off the sprue using a sharp craft knife (or a razor saw if the sprue is particularly thick). This will put you firmly in control of the removal process and will, if you do it correctly, just leave a little excess plastic needing to

be tidied up. In some cases it may possible to cut the part cleanly from sprue to leave a nice tidy line that ne no further attention. Realistically, in m situations, the best way is actually to c little way out from the edge of the with the first cut and them to trim remainder of the waste material near the finished line. The resulting 'pip' then be smoothed down by gently rub it down with a few strokes of a small needle file.

Once all of the parts have removed, it is time to have a dry-ru the assembly process. A dry-run, fo

Once again the small, flat needle file comes in handy for this. All you have to do is to make a few gentle strokes with the file, check to see if the parts are a better fit and repeat the process a time or two until the problem with the poorly fitting joint is resolved. It may sound obvious but I was taught that it is better to take off a little at a time rather than to go mad and file away too much in one go that you can't, of course, put back later.

Now we can start the assembly process for real. One of the reasons I chose the Dapol cottage for a beginner's kit is that the main parts are designed to fit together in perfect alignment by means of integral blocks and strips on the insides of the corner joints. If you look carefully at the illustrations you will see that the right angle joint between adjacent sides comprises a mitre and raised plastic mouldings. Unlike a typical mitred joint, these raised strips locate the parts and also prevent the possibility of the joint slipping or sliding around as the parts are held together. All you need to do in practice is to line up the top and bottom of each joint, add some glue and hold it together for a short while until the glue has had time to hold things together.

1. The Dapol thatched cottage in bits.

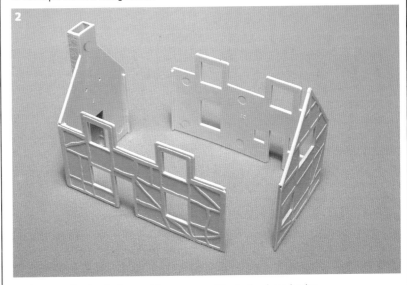

2. The two wall and end sub assemblies are seen waiting for the glue to harden.

...nitiated, is basically a familiarisation ...rcise so that enables you to see just ...w the parts fit together and make ...rself aware of the sequence of ...embly before any adhesive is used. ...suming that you have already read ...ough the instructions before starting ...k, this should only take a minute or ... and hopefully will present no real ...blems at all.

...lthough it wasn't necessary with the ...ol kits you see here, you do sometimes ... that the dry-run highlights little ...ustments that need to be made to ...st the fitting of the parts together.

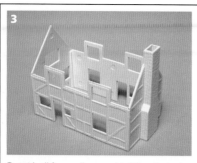

3. With all four walls, assembled the attached chimney stack can be seen on one end.

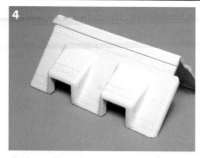

4. The roof is made up of a ridge and two slopes.

5. Next, the roof is fixed to the walls.

6. A pastel base colour is applied as painting gets under way.

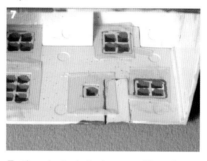

7. Clear plastic glazing is cut roughly to size and is glued in place behind the windows.

8. Strips of coloured paper are added to represent curtains.

In common with more or less any polystyrene kit, the best adhesive by far to use is a liquid polystyrene cement such as Slater's Mek Pak. You can, if you prefer, still use that good old-fashioned stuff in a tube, but its stringy properties and propensity to dispense onto the parts far too thickly, really makes it a non-starter for most modellers these days. Liquid solvent as it is often called is much more user-friendly, it is non-stringy and can be put exactly where you want it. Simply load your brush and apply it to the back of the joint which has already been brought together. The liquid will then run into the joint and will spread by capillary action. When you are happy that just enough solvent has been applied, simply keep holding things together for a while as the quick-drying liquid does its job.

While the joint is setting you can quickly check that it is a good right angle by offering up an engineer's square if you have one. If you don't have one you can still check things are ok by sight or use an old dodge - just sit the joint on a sheet of lined exercise paper such that the right

angle between the feint and margin act as your 90° guide lines.

With two walls attached to each other, the second pairing will literally be a piece of cake. Yes, you've guessed, the process is a carbon copy of what you've just done with the first ones. As the glue dries, it is worth noting that I haven't stuck the windows in prior to assembly in this instance, largely as it will be easier to paint them before fitting them later in the assembly process. If, as can often be experienced in much more complicated kits, window fixing is going to be too awkward at a later stage, I would recommend that the windows are painted first and are attached to the flat parts prior to assembly.

The next task is to bring together the two wall sub-assembles to make the basic rectangular cottage structure. One again try the parts without adding solvent first. Hopefully, if your right angles are true, the two joints will be a perfect fit and all you will have to do is to run in a little liquid solvent into each joint. Although I found no problems at all with this cottage,

some kits do require a bit of fitting a light filing to assist the assembly proce You will soon be able to tell if any needed and will be able to judge thin based on your newly found model maki experience.

Being of a very simple nature, t cottage's mock thatched roof compris just three parts, namely the two slop and a ridge section that the two slopes into. Essentially all you have to do her to fit and glue one of the slopes into ridge, (you will see exactly where slope goes as it has a small mould rebate on its upper edge). When this dry, just repeat exactly the same proc with the other roof slope and it's done.

Before the roof can be fixed crown the walls, there is a one-piece ste chimney stack that needs to be glued place on one end walls. Once is attached, the roof should drop stra down onto the walls without any need filing or modification whatsoever. A spots of solvent applied from inside model with soon have the roof fi firmly in place once and for all.

In order that I could fit the windows on my model, I now had to paint the kit. My preference for plastic kits is to use matt enamel paints such as those in the Humbrol, Revell or Precision ranges. In this case the plan of attack is to firstly paint the rendered panels between the cottage's timber framework with a lighter pastel shade. Having left this for 24 hours to dry thoroughly, the offensive continues by picking out the raised timbers with a greyish brown to represent the darker treated wood. Don't worry too much if you think that this is too difficult to do. Try holding a fine paintbrush at a very flat angle to the wall, and paint using its side (just behind the tip) rather than with the tip itself as you would do when holding it at 90 or 60 degrees to the wall. Hopefully the paint will then only be applied to the raised surface of the framing and not on the panelling at the same time. If, as is possible, a bit of paint does go astray, just let it dry and go over the background and touch in the affected area.

A common perception is that thatched roofs should be painted a yellowy straw colour which in reality is only found on freshly thatched properties. Look around you and you will find that thatch weathers quite rapidly to a much darker brownie-black colour. Bearing this in mind, I used Humbrol matt dark earth M29 as a basis and streaked in a little black as the paint was starting to dry, with a touch of colour to the stonework around the chimney. The windows could then be inserted into the apertures on the walls and the job as they say is a good 'un.

To complete each window, you will need to solvent-weld the moulding into the aperture and then add a rectangle of clear plastic glazing on the inside of the model behind the window frame to represent the glass. A nice finishing touch is to make and add dummy curtains from strips of painted plastic card or coloured paper as and when required.

Having completed a first fairly basic kit, it is worth mentioning that there are a couple of improvements that can be made to almost any plastic kit like this.

The first option is to add internal walls and floors to divide up the open space such that you can't see all the way through to the other side when you look in through the windows. These can be quickly made up from either scraps of sturdy card or from plastic card sheet.

Secondly, if you intend to light up your model when it is fixed down on the layout you will be well advised to line the walls or paint the inside of the model black. Being rather thin and less than opaque, the polystyrene walls and roof will readily let light through them rather than just allowing it to pass through the windows as you really want. I remember as a child having the same old Airfix buildings (now manufactured by Dapol) on my train set being lined with old cereal boxes and tin foil for this very reason. It may have been a cheap and cheerful dodge with it worked very well indeed!

completed cottage kit.

Dapol's country church.

Dapol Country Church

For our second, slightly more difficult, example of an unpainted kit we can follow the various stages of assembly needed to construct Dapol's small but distinctive country church kit.

Here as with the cottage we follow the same basic processes of removing the parts, having a dry-run and sticking things together before painting the whole thing ready for use on the layout. Being a little more involved it is worth spending a few more minutes reading and studying the drawings and instructions that accompany the kit. If you take a look at the photos you will see that the construction process isn't perhaps as daunting to the beginner as it might at first seem. Indeed, in reality, assembly breaks down into several relatively easy to handle stages that, given a little patience and enthusiasm, will soon reward you with a very useful completed model.

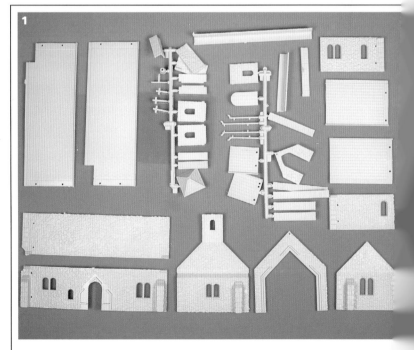

1. The kit as you buy it.

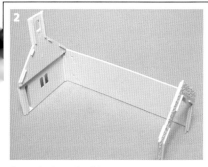

2. Firstly, the ends of the main section are added to the back.

3. The front wall completes the building of this element.

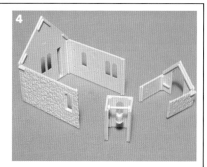

4. The bell tower, porch and smaller extension are made up in isolation as sub-assemblies.

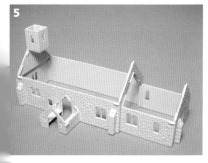

5 These are then added to the main section of the church.

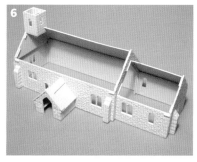

6. Next, the first roof slopes are fixed in place.

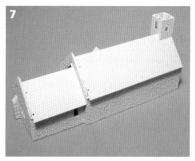

7. The same stage as 6 seen from the reverse angle.

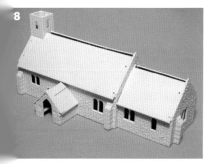

. The addition of the remaining roof sections e the church take shape.

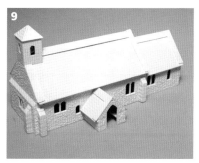

9. A ridge, stonework copings and the bell tower roof complete the construction process.

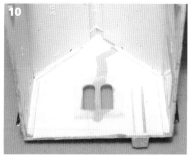

10. Glazing is attached to the inside of the church windows.

11. The church completed by the addition of the rainwater pipes after painting.

Hornby Pub

Adding to the multitude of plastic kits manufactured for the railway modeller, we find a small number of models that, although essentially are pre-coloured construction kits, contain certain parts that are a departure from the norm. In an attempt to realistically replicate subtle stonework details and complex colouration, some kits employ printed full colour, self-adhesive overlays. Thankfully these sheets come ready cut out so that they can be peeled straight off the backing sheet and are immediately ready to use. Incidentally, the pub shown here, although marketed by Hornby, was actually marked and manufactured by the popular producer of continental kits, Pola. Now, I know that the more informed reader will quickly point out that Hornby have now discontinued kits like these from their latest catalogue but, in fairness to others who may have this type of kit stashed away in their 'future projects' drawer or simply pick one up from a second-hand stall, I think it is still

Ready for business, the pub is complete.

relevant and well worth giving them a mention in this publication.

From a construction perspective, the only real difference is that the walls are

moulded in flat unfinished (but st coloured) plastic and have to be overla with the printed paper sheets. Simp you might think. Well, yes it is up to

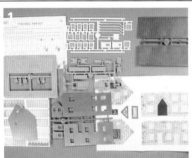

1. The contents of the kit.

2. The first corner is stuck together.

3. Windows and doors are added from the inside of the model.

4. The self adhesive pre-printed overlay quickly transforms the appearance of the walls.

5. With the two wall/end sub-assemblies stuck together the building starts to take shape.

6. A small thatched porch is built up next ar is added to the front wall.

point, but you do have the added complication that all of the window and door apertures on the overlay need to be lined up precisely with the corresponding openings on the plastic parts. I will readily admit to having to carefully peel off one half-attached overlay from a plastic side while making up one of these models as it became obvious that things were not going to end up quite in alignment. The lesson I learnt was to start in the middle of the sheet and to slowly work outwards one half at a time.

Another thing to look out for while attaching the overlay is to avoid trapping pockets of air or bubbles forming between the plastic and its paper covering. Simply work outwards as you firmly press down and smooth the overlay onto the wall just as you would do when you hang wallpaper, in effect forcing out any trapped air in so doing.

Perhaps it is also worth noting that excessive handing of the self-adhesive side of the overlay can result in the mock stone layer not sticking down too well or in some circumstances not at all. If you experience this, all is not lost. Just lift the offending area of overlay with the tip of a modelling knife blade and brush on a liberal amount of liquid polystyrene cement. While the surface of the plastic is still nice and tacky, simply press the overlay down and smooth it into position as before. If you wish you could soak the paper with a bit more solvent from outside the stone layer but be careful not to damage or remove the printed surface. If you have any doubts, try the solvent on a scrap of printed material or an area of the model that will eventually be hidden from view.

As you can see from this section, plastic kits are an excellent way of both adding lineside interest and for developing your modelling skills. With this in mind we will, a little later in this book, take a look at some other types of plastic kits including some that are specifically aimed at the modern image modeller.

7. The basic roof structure is fixed together ensuring that the angle between the two pitches is the same as the apex of the wall's gable end.

8. To this the gutters are added along the eaves at the bottom of the slopes.

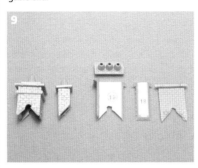

9. Chimneys are then assembled separately from the roof.

10. The chimneys are then glued in place on top of the roof.

11. Small rectangles of plastic glazing are cut out and attached behind the windows.

12. The window detailing is completed by the addition of printed paper curtains.

13. With the roof now stuck down on top of the walls, construction is nearing completion.

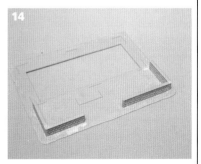

14. A plastic base with walls comes in the kit as an optional feature.

Dapol's semi-detached house.

If your modelling preferences cover more recent times, you will, no doubt, be looking to populate the layout with suitable residential properties of the period. Some of the best, and more widely available examples, fall into the plastic construction kit category as produced by the likes of Dapol and up until recently, Hornby. Perhaps the big advantage of using plastic kits for housing is that, being cheap, quick, and easy to make, they can readily made in multiples to accurately reflect estate housing of the modern age.

With the assembly process being, as with most other plastic kits covered by this book, very straightforward indeed, there is little more to add here that hasn't already been said earlier. It is, however, well worth photographically following a few worked examples from the box to the baseboard to illustrate some of the kits that you can buy.

Dapol Semi-detached Houses

This pair of houses represents one of the most common types of property found in this country, the ubiquitous semi-detached house. Looking to me like a product of the post second world war 1950s or 1960s, the architectural style suggests that they are more like to be private occupancy rather than the 'council' (or should I now s 'social'?) variety. A simple change door type and some good old-fashior small-paned 'Crittal' metal windo would soon convert them to the latte you fancy modifying them a bit.

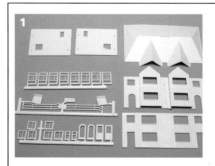

1. The un-built kit.

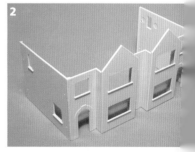

2. The end walls are fixed to the front.

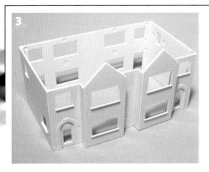

3. The completed wall assembly.

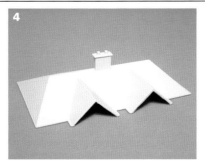

4. The roof and chimney stack.

5. The basic shell ready for painting.

6. The main colours have been applied prior to fitting of the windows.

7. The windows glazing and paper curtains have been stuck in place.

apol Detached House

is suburban detached dwelling is tty typical of any suburban setting across the country. Judging by its appearance I would reckon that the prototype would have been built between the 1930s and 1950s but would suit layouts based on periods much later than that.

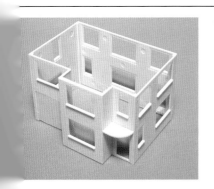

The walls have all been glued together.

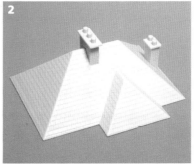

2. The roof is made up separately.

3. Dapol's detached house nears completion.

Hornby Georgian House

With architecture much later than the Dapol kits, this mock Georgian detached house is very typical of the 1970s and 1980s and comes with a garage that can be attached to the property or left free-standing.

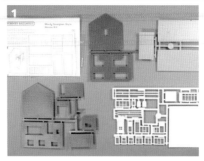

1. The unbuilt kit.

2. The first two walls are fixed together.

3. The first floor strengthens the assembly.

4. The garage is built up separately.

5. The two sub-assemblies together.

6. Windows and doors are added next.

7. Close up of the window detail.

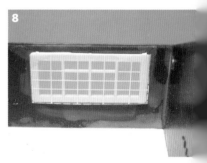

8. Glazing is fixed behind the window frame.

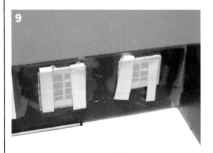

9. Paper curtains are then added.

10. The completed garage.

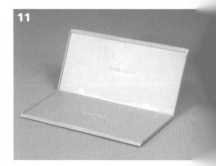

11. The roof comprises two parts.

Hornby's Georgian-style house

This modern house is another kit from Hornby.

Three views of Uffington signal box which is of a similar but slightly smaller design than the Dapol kit.

As a child I fondly remember travelling by train from Peterborough to Leicester and being shown upon arrival at Oakham, the prototype that inspired the 'Airfix signal box'. Although Oakham's celebrity box has received some modernisation and modification over the years it still stands guard over the level crossing on the main road at the end of the platform.

Just like its real-life version, this easy-to-build kit is still going strong but is now manufactured by Dapol and not Airfix. Differing in size but of same general design, the two ot signal boxes depicted, at Uffington Ketton on the same line, have g kit-bashing potential for the rail modeller who could easily use Dapol kit as a starting point.

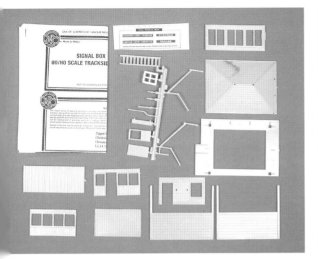

he Dapol Oakham signal box kit.

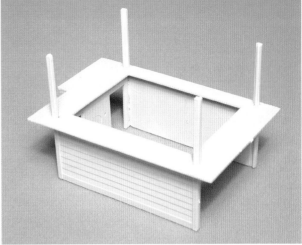

Stage one - the base fits into the walkway.

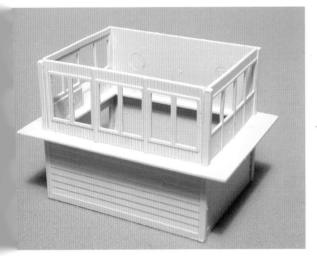

upper structure is added.

Almost finished and ready for painting.

amous Oakham level crossing signal box.

Ketton is a larger variant of the Midland signal box design.

In addition to both card and plastic building kits, ones made from a plaster-based material also prove particularly popular with railway modellers who want something that looks pretty realistic yet is relatively simple to assemble.

As with other sections of this book, we aught to take a quick run down of the basic stages of construction. They are : -

- Carefully unwrapping the parts from the packaging to prevent damage
- Familiarisation with the parts and instructions
- Assembly of the building
- Painting

To commence our review of this kit type we will start by constructing a typical plaster cast kit, in this case, the ubiquitous terraced house, before taking a look at a 7mm scale platelayers' hut. We conclude the section with a few more plaster examples to offer the newcomer a little food for thought.

Townstreet Terrace

When you get your parcel from Townstreet it is just like Christmas. Each casting comes individually wrapped in loads of newspaper to prevent damage in transit.

Having disposed of the scrap

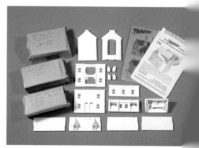

The castings as they come from the packaging

newsprint into the re-cycling bin, can see that the complete version typical terraced house comprises thirteen parts, and that includes chimneys and the extension at the

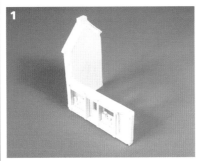

1. Firstly, the lower half of a shop front is glued to an end wall.

2. The upper half is then added.

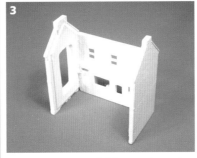

3. An intermediate wall follows ready to take the adjoining building.

4. The three parts to the back extension are stuck together.

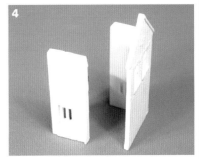

5. These are allowed to dry before being offered up to the back wall.

6. This close up shows just how easy it is to add simple curtains to the windows.

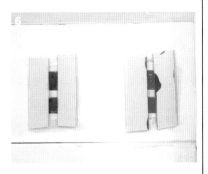

7. With the back wall added to the shop, the neighbouring house is ready to be fixed in place.

8. The addition of the roof slopes sees the structure nearing completion.

completed terraced street.

he parts as we have become to ect from Townstreet are very cleanly t in 'Chrystacast', a very fine k-hard plaster from British Gypsum. might find that one or two parts ht need a quick touch with a small or some fine wet and dry paper to oth off any flash left from the ing process, but it only takes a few onds to do and is, after all, no real lem to do at all.

s you can see from the accompanying es of photos, the construction ess is very simple and ghtforward in keeping with

10. Nearing completion, the low relief row is seen during painting.

11. A close up of the Ironmonger's Shop interior shows off its fine cast detail.

Townstreet's policy to make their kits suitable for modellers of all capabilities. The glue used to hold things together is good old-fashioned white PVA adhesive spread liberally onto the parts before they are positioned together. Rather than go mad and stick everything together in one hit, I tend to take the more cautious approach and let individual sub-assemblies dry thoroughly before adding the next section as the building takes shape.

It is probably worth mentioning that you do need to supply and add you own glazing and curtains behind the cast windows in some locations before final assembly as you will have great difficulty in so doing once the basic shell is complete. I find that rectangles of plastic glazing are probably best fixed to the plaster using Evo-stick solvent-free contact adhesive as are the pre-painted strips of 20 thou plastic card that are ideal for representing the curtains.

If you are interested in just how b﹖ these houses are, I have checked th﹖ leading dimensions and report that th﹖ individual shop or house unit is 115m﹖ long and 140mm high with widt﹖ varying from a mere 37mm for t﹖ low-relief example to 74mm on the f﹖ house with a plain back, and 106m﹖ where the full house has a ba﹖ extension. Although I haven't got o﹖ to measure, a quick calculation sugge﹖ that the optional low-relief versi﹖ featuring a house back with

An example of the prototype – who put that in﹖ This isn't a prototype inspiration page! Photo: Keith Parkinson.

extension would be approximately 69mm wide.

As far as painting goes, the white plaster finish lends itself to being washed with matt enamels mixed from colours in the Humbrol, Phoenix Precision and J. Perkins ranges, suitably thinned with white spirit. Although I haven't emphasised it in this instance, the deep joints cast between the bricks of Townstreet's components are ideal to show off a contrasting mortar colour. Once the walls have been painted with a base colour of matt enamel, simply brush the surface of the painted walls with a generous coat of water making sure that it goes into all of the joints. Then, before the water dries out, take a very weak mix of grey (thinned white emulsion with a few spots of black and a spot or two of washing up liquid to reduce the surface tension), load your brush and simply touch the wall where a number of bricks meet. Capillary action instantaneously draws the grey paint quite a way into the dampened joints. To cover a whole building you have to repeat the process several times, wiping away any excess paint as you go along.

Once the brick walls have been painted, the fine detailing can be simply picked out using a small, good quality brush. This can take a little while to do, so just take your time and enjoy it.

n Commandments LNER
ut

isn't just Townstreet that produce ding kits from the plaster medium. ns such as the interestingly-named Commandments also use this erial for their models and essories. In this instance the subject 7mm scale version of the same ER platelayers hut that they also duce in 2mm and 4mm scales.

s you can see, the pre-cast concrete ototype lends itself well to the cast roach and is indeed very easy to put ther. Construction, as you might ect, follows the same basic processes sed for the Townstreet kits.

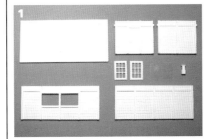

1. The kit of parts.

2. The first wall/end sub-assembly.

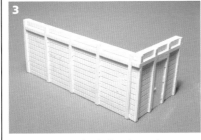

3. This is repeated with the other end.

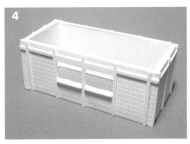

4. The two sub-assemblies are brought

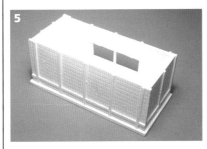

5. The roof is added and is left upside down to dry.

6. The hut takes shape

7. The completed 7mm scale platelayers' hut.

Set in a rural scene, the painted cottage is set off with a few simply made garden plants and shrubs.

Townstreet Cottage

Measuring approximately 130mm x 85mm x 114mm high, this cottage kit, in keeping with Townstreet's proven philosophy, is very simple indeed comprising just six plaster castings that can be supplemented by some etched brass frets for the windows.

1. The castings as they come.

2. A view of a wall section from behind showing the various stages of window construction and the addition of the curtains.

3. The first three walls are assembled ready to take the fourth.

4. The two assemblies for the walls and the roof.

4. Assembly complete, the cottage is ready f painting.

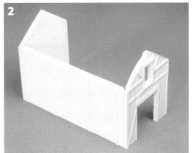

1. Under construction - assembly of the plaster walls takes shape.

2. Rustic and rural – the completed barn,

Sheds and Barns.

These small but very useful little buildings are ideal for adding interest to the station scene or rural diorama. They also make ideal starter kits for the beginner.

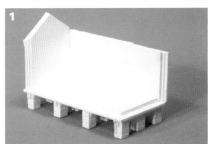

1. Under construction.

2. The completed shed poses for the camera.

Townstreet Sand Building

One of the latest additions to the Townstreet range is this unusual lineside building complete with brick chimney. Used in engine shed areas for drying locomotive sand, this model complements the steam motive power depot scene.

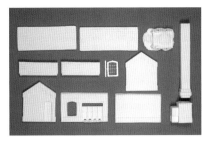

The bits!

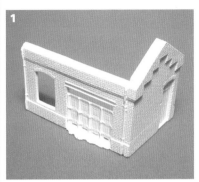

1. Assembly begins in the usual way.

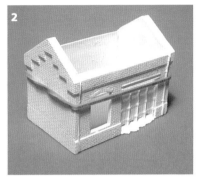

2. Rubber bands are ideal for holding the parts together as the glue dries.

3. The two-piece roof is added next.

4. A clerestory roof vent is positioned on top of the roof.

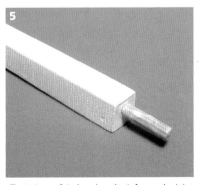

5. A piece of timber dowel reinforces the joint between the chimney and its base.

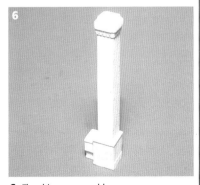

6. The chimney assembly.

mpleted sand building.

LMS 'Jubilee' 4-6-0 *Leander* poses in front of the coaling tower at Carnforth in 1979. Photo: Brian Sharpe.

If you are planning to build a steam-era engine shed on your layout, a coaling tower similar to this one might feature prominently in your plans. Built mainly from reinforced concrete, coaling towers were once one of the most impressive and fascinating civil engineering structures seen along the lineside. Largely due to their considerable size they are rarely modelled. In an attempt to redress the balance, Townstreet have produced this easy-to-assemble plaster kit that, once built, needs only painting to finish it off. Although the kit is primarily intended as a static feature, I am sure some enterprising model maker will motorise one before too long!

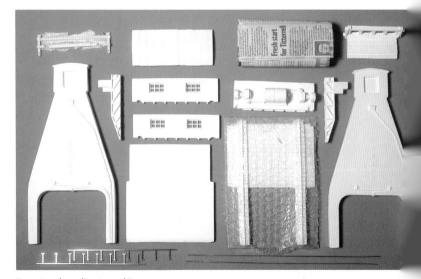

Townstreet's coaling tower kit.

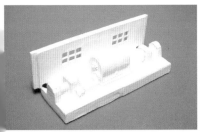

The inside of the motor room.

The kit is seen during assembly.

Above: The completed coaling tower.

Left: The underside of the tower reveals the coal chutes.

Below: This coaling stage is at Immingham. Photo: Brian Sharpe.

LANGLEY MASTERBUILD KITS

If you have ever visited Langley Miniature Models website or have wandered into their impressive stand at exhibitions, you will, I am certain, have found it to be an Aladdin's cave of all kinds of scenic components and accessories. Although perhaps more famously known for their extensive range of cast whitemetal figures, road vehicles and fairground kits, Langley also manufacture a series of highly-detailed, easy-to-assemble low-relief building kits.

Retailed under the Masterbuild label, the range includes such niceties as lineside warehouses, shops, house fronts and backs, retaining walls and railway arches, together with a useful collection of bridge and tunnel mouths These kits come in a complete but fairly basic form which can, if the individual chooses, be supplemented by the comprehensive collection of detailing packs that are also available. In this way

Victorian Villas Langley style – the scene is completed by a
passing bus which incidentally also heralds from the Langley range.

the builder can pick and mix exactly what optional extra embellishments, if any, he or she wants to add without having to spend more money up front on components that may well be discarded later.

The spin off of all of these supplementary packs is that all of the component parts included in these kits are available separately to kit-bashers and scratch-builders like me. If you would like to know just what goodies you can get to use or adapt in your own

models, Langley have produced a useful handbook dedicated to this range. In it you get comprehensive instructions and tips on how to build these models as well as illustrations of the full range and listings of exactly what is available individually.

As the construction process is pretty much unique to kits in this range, it is perhaps a good idea to follow the construction of one of Langley's Victorian Terraced Villa Fronts. In its basic form, this kit comprises transparent PVC vacuum formings for the row of four villa fronts, a separate forming for the front gardens/pavements and curtains; etched-brass parts for the windows and doors and whitemetal castings for the bay windows and the decorative surrounds to all other windows and doors. The villas are actually designed, if the builder so chooses, to be super-detailed by the addition of such items as barge boards, rainwater pipes and gutters, railings gates and posts, and a host of sundry details which Langley supply as optional extras. Once completed, you will have a low-relief model to fit against the backscene that measures a reasonable 373mm long x 70mm deep x 110mm high.

Having decided not to super-detail the model for the purposes of this exercise, it is now time to make a start. The first job as I am sure you have already guessed, is to carefully cut around the PVC moulding that forms the villa fronts using a sharp craft knife i.e. one with a new blade. I know that I usually advocate using a steel straight edge for cutting all straight lines but in this case the relief of the forming prevents one from being used and makes this situation an exception to the rule. This being the case, it is necessary to cut freehand around the perimeter of the elevation, taking each cut very steadily indeed. You need to trim the material with just enough pressure on the blade so as to cut cleanly without distorting the wall forming which could easily cause the blade to stray from the desired line.

As always I think that it is best to practise a little first. Try a few cuts on a scrap of the waste PVC if you are not too confident. Better still, cut out the curtains and paving/garden parts first and you will soon get used to material's flexible characteristics and the way that it cuts. Don't forget to use a cutting mat if you have one. Never cut on a wooden surface that has loads of old cutting marks or a grain such as plywood for this is a sure recipe for disaster as the blade will undoubtedly get trapped in a groove and will readily wander off all over the place, taking your nice straight line with it.

As you handle the PVC mouldings you will soon see that they are quite flexible and will benefit greatly from some form of stiffening and support. Indeed, Langley, recommends that the model is strengthened before it is fixed in its final position and, to this end, supply paper templates for all of the plastic card parts that are needed to reinforce the structure. These templates can either be used as a guide for marking out (or for sticking to) sheets of 40 – 60 thou plastic card (which are not supplied in the kit) prior to them being cut out with a sharp craft knife. Once made, these stiffeners need to be checked for clearance by dry-fitting in place on the model. When you are happy they are a good fit and are clear of the windows, you can stick them permanently in place behind the walls. Even though you could probably build this kit with little or no support whatsoever and stick it straight down onto the baseboard and backscene, I still think it is well worth making the extra effort, particularly as in the end, you will finish up with a much stronger structure that is less likely to move or twist in the heat of a hot summer.

From a model maker's perspective, perhaps one of the most difficult things about this kit is not in its construction but is actually in making the right choice of adhesive for fixing the various types of materials to one another. Sticking similar materials together is pretty easy but whenever you have unmatched parts such as plastic and metal, the choice always becomes that little bit more difficult. I always suggest that the best way of making this decision if you are uncertain is to try out various glues on scraps of the materials being used. In the end I chose to use: -

- Mek Pak liquid polystyrene cement for plastic card to plastic card joints
- Contact adhesive such as solvent-free Evo-stik for sticking the plastic card strengthening pieces to the PVC wall moulding
- Epoxy resin for attaching the windows and their surrounds to the walls
- Superglue for making up the bay window surrounds.

Having said all that, I am not entirely convinced that the choice of using epoxy to stick metal to plastic was the right one. I know the manufacturer recommends it in the instructions but, from experience I also am aware that if the plastic flexes or you drop the completed model in transit, the epoxy joint is likely to come, away taking with it any paint behind. As an alternative and, in hindsight, I would probably now use the solvent-free version of contact adhesive, largely as it is so sticky and clingy and is unlikely to come undone under similar circumstances.

With the wall forming firmly stuck to the paving/garden forming and having attached all of the strengthening pieces,

we can now apply the basic colours onto the walls, before we make the painting process more difficult than it would be once all of the detailing is added. As you can see from the photos, I chose to paint the villas in three shades using various mixes of matt enamels which seemed to cover the PVC reasonably well without the need for a primer. Having firstly painted the outer houses different colours and let them dry thoroughly, I simply applied neatly cut strips of masking tape to the walls to get a reasonably straight line between neighbouring houses before I painted the middle one yet another shade. While I had got the paints out, it seemed pretty logical to paint the roof as well and, once again to make the model look more interesting, chose two apply two different shades of grey to adjoining areas of the slate roof before weathering it in places to give it an impression of age.

As the paint dries on the walls, the rest of the parts can be prepared in readiness for final assembly. The windows and doors supplied in this kit comprise an etched-brass fret that represents the timber sash window frame with its glazing bars, and a cast whitemetal surround which forms the decorative masonry embellishment that is often found on buildings of this era. As with other kits of this type, I found that these parts needed a little judicious cleaning up before they were ready to fit into the pre-formed apertures in the PVC wall

moulding. In particular some of the brass windows needed to be filed top and bottom to help them sit snugly in place against the glazing. If you haven't tried something like this before don't be put off. A little fettling and tweaking is often needed when kit-building but, believe you me, you will always be pleased that you have spent those few extra minutes when it fits together neatly and you stand back and admire your completed model.

Although the first floor windows and doors are pretty much ready to fit, the bay windows on the ground floor do necessitate a bit more attention prior to fixing in place. Firstly, the etched parts need to be folded using the half etched lines so that the two sides of the bay are at an angle to the larger central window section. To determine the correct angle, simply offer up the etch to the wall moulding, check the fitting and adjust as many times as necessary until you have a window that follows the lines of the moulding perfectly. In front of the window etching is an ornate decorative Victorian surround which comprises three whitemetal parts that have to be stuck together exactly the correct angle to each other. I actually tried two ways of doing this, the first was using low-melt solder (see the section on whitemetal building kits for more details about this) and the second using a thick cyanoacrylate adhesive such as Roket Max. Although

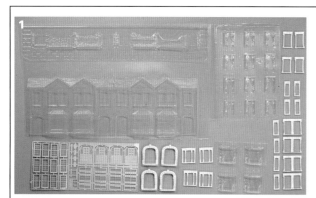
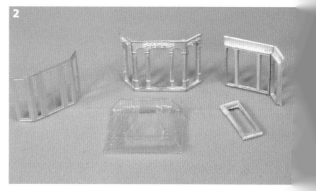

1. The kit in bits, note the clear forming that avoids the need for glazing the windows.

2. Bay window construction showing the part built components, and the completed bay window surround

usually solder almost anything made of whitemetal, I found getting the angle right between parts to be particularly fiddly in this instance. When I tried superglueing the second surround together and got good results straight away, my mind was instantly made up. The remaining two surrounds were similarly glued together as a matter of course and the soldering iron was quickly put away.

As bought, the window etching represents typical Victorian sash windows that are divided up into a lot of small individual glass panes. You can, if you wish, add a bit of variety to your own building by making a simple modification or two to the windows in one or more of the houses. If you look carefully at the photographs you will see that I have taken the snippers and file to a small number of the windows and have removed the glazing bars to all of the smaller panes leaving just one central vertical bar in place. This remaining glazing bar could also be snipped out in a similar way to make yet another more modern looking variant of the house type which has obviously had replacement window frames fitted at some point in its history.

Now that the parts for the windows and doors have been prepared, the next task is to prime both the brass and whitemetal components. The best way of doing this in no time at all, I find, is to use a white aerosol spray car primer. Once left to dry and harden overnight they can be painted with contrasting matt enamels to the walls in readiness for assembly.

As I have already said my piece on the subject of glues and adhesives, all I really need to note now is that once the etched parts have been secured in place in the window recesses, the surrounds have to be glued in position above them. Having already cut out and painted the moulded curtains and fitted them ready for use, these can also be attached to the back of the walls behind the windows.

3. The villa back is easily strengthened by fixing plastic card in place behind the PVC forming

4. The etched window frames are fitted into rebates in the walls.

5. This photo shows the etched frame from the front elevation.

6. Finally, the pre-painted whitemetal surrounds are added to complete the model.

Finally, to complete the model all you need to do is to add a bit more paint to pick out various fine details such as the pavements and gardens, lightly weather the building with judicious dry-brushing or weathering powders and perhaps add a bit of scenic material and a bush or two to complete the scene.

Although these kits may seem a little on the expensive side for some modellers, it is well worth remembering that they do contain a large number of good quality etched and cast parts. Having tried this example, I certainly think the Masterbuild kit range are easy to make and are well worth considering when you start planning your next layout. With components available too, you might just want to make light work of those ornate windows and doors or awkward-to-make fittings when you next scratch-build a building.

Dunster station from the station approach

Travel just a few miles inland by steam, or for that matter heritage diesel traction, from the West Somerset Railway's Minehead headquarters and you will find the peaceful country station at Dunster. Perhaps better known to tourists for its historic hilltop castle and ancient yarn market, Dunster is also the inspiration for the Hornby station kit of the same name. Although this kit is now withdrawn from the catalogue, I have still seen examples on sale both in model shops and on club sales stands and so is still worth a quick look. The 4mm scale plastic kit is itself very easy to put together and features self-adhesive pre-coloured printed stonework overlays similar to the pub kit featured earlier. As you can see from the view looking across the platform, Dunster's setting amongst the trees forms a super scenic break making it an ideal candidate for a sm Western Region country station.

Dunster's tree lined setting makes a splendid layout idea.

nster station – the model.

arly stage of assembly.

The walls and windows are complete.

at roof and copings are added.

The platform elevation.

The completed 7mm scale NMB Models GWR corrugated platform goods shed from Skytrex in a rural setting.

Having never attempted to build up a resin kit before I started working on this book, I was particularly interested if not intrigued to see just how they go together. My guinea pigs in this instance were three of a wide range of 7mm scale kits that originally formed the NMB range and are now available from Skytrex of Loughborough. Firstly, we will review a simple lineside lamp hut before building a typical station news stand and finally attempt something a little more complicated in the shape of a small corrugated goods shed.

Generally I would say that if you are happy putting together plastic kits, you would find no great problems assembling resin parts so long as you remember that –

- Resin is much more brittle than plastic
- Parts are less forgiving when bent and can crack if you are not careful
- A little more cleaning up/preparation is needed prior to assembly
- The adhesives used are not quite as simple to work with
- The casting process can leave some parts a little distorted

Two types of adhesive are recommended in the instructions for these kits, namely rapid-drying epoxy resin and superglue. I tried both in the interests of science as they say and found that the two-part epoxy resin such as Araldite Rapid is best suited to the larger joints such as those in the corners of the buildings. In these cases, an element of filling is often required

and it is sometimes beneficial to be a[ble] to move the parts around for a min[ute] or two as you ensure that you ha[ve] everything perfectly aligned before [the] glue finally goes off. Superglue, on [the] other hand, is probably best suited [to] fixing together some of the sma[ller] parts such as windows, doors and [the] like.

If you do find distortion in any of [the] resin parts, the instructions suggest [that] there is an easy solution to the prob[lem,] simply boil the kettle and carefully p[our] a little boiling water over the affe[cted] area. With the resin softened, the [part] can be readily manipulated unti[l the] original shape has been reforme[d. I] tried this for myself and am please[d to] report that I soon had things bac[k to] normal again.

Lamp Hut

Having unpacked the box and examined the resin castings, you will soon find that, although the parts are neatly and cleanly moulded, you will at first need to spend a few minutes tidying them up before you can start assembly. In this case I found that a small amount of resin 'flash' from the casting process needed to be removed from the window and door openings using a small, flat-sided needle file. In addition I felt it necessary to carefully file and fine-tune the mitred angles at the building's corners in an effort to ensure that they make nice neat right-angled joints when they are eventually glued together using quick-setting Araldite Rapid.

As illustrated, assembly is very straight forward following the standard, stick one end to a side wall, repeat with the second pairing and then bring the two sub-assembles together, process.

Unlike the cast resin walls, the hut's roof is made from a rectangle of embossed corrugated plastic card that needs to be shaped to the correct curvature and then trimmed to size. To do this, you firstly need to find a solid object, preferably one that won't melt, having roughly the same diameter as the roof's curve. Having offered one of the end walls up to countess household objects, I eventually found a small glass jam jar that was an exact fit. Next, wrap the sheet of plastic around the jar (ensuring in so doing that the corrugations line up across the finished roof) and hold it in place with a couple of rubber bands. Now boil a kettle and pour boiling water over the whole thing. With the plastic sufficiently softened it just needs to be held firmly in place against the former so that as it cools it take up its new curved shape. As Araldite isn't really suitable for sticking plastic card to resin, I used Evo-Stik solvent-free contact adhesive instead.

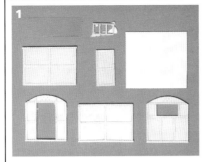

1. The kit of parts displayed.

2. Two walls are glued together.

3. As are the other two walls.

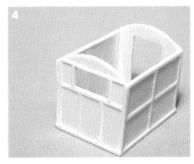

4. The four walls make up the hut's basic box structure.

5. An old jar makes an ideal former for the curved roof.

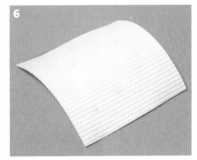

6. The curved corrugated roof after treating with boiling water.

7. The completed hut ready for primer and painting.

Bookstall

Slightly more complicated than the lamp hut, this typical platform-mounted news stand has a few more parts and involves some tricky irregular angles on the front wall to put together.

Just as we have seen with the hut, construction starts with the filing, fitting and glueing of the flat back wall to the two small end section that sit perpendicular to it. While this is hardening, the three front wall sections, yes the ones that are at funny angles, can be considered. Rather than attempt to set out the angles by eye, I decided to be a bit more scientific and elected to draw out the actual floor plan, angles and all, full size on a sheet of paper. Knowing the exact measurements of the back section that has already been glued, and with the lengths of the other three bits to measure off, it didn't take long to arc off the lengths with a pair of compasses and draw in the front wall parallel to the back one. OK, so this might at first seem a lot of unnecessary messing around but we now have a simple but accurate template which will enable the awkward angles to be set up without fuss or guesswork whatsoever.

With planning complete, the next job is to bring two wall sections together and check that they are a good fit. After a bit of judicious filework to ensure that the angles make a tidy joint, they can be glued together using the paper template as a setting-out guide. Now you do need to hold the angled joint in place without it slipping out of true for a while as the glue sets; just be a little patient and you will soon have the pleasure of repeating the process with the second angle.

Here on in construction is a doddle. The two sub-assemblies, once fitted, are fixed together, the small counters can be superglued in place and the roof with its hoarding is simply stuck on top of the walls.

Being prototypically wooden, I decided to give the news stand a varnished teak finish. To do this I gave the primed resin surface a streaky coat of matt tan (Humbrol M62 or M63 will do this) making sure that the streaks follow the grain of the wooden members. When this is dry, a second streaky coat of paint is applied but using a rich chestnut colour on this occasion. To bring out the timber effect the model is left to dry again before final coat of satin varnish is applied.

Finally, before the model is ready for fitting out with papers, people and posters, a couple of rectangles of clear plastic glazing can be fixed behind the display windows using contact adhesive and a small nail can be fitted to the door as its handle.

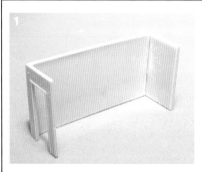

1. Firstly, the two end walls are fixed to the back.

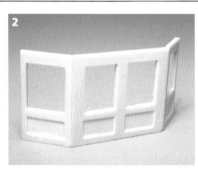

2. Having made a template to ensure the angles are correct, the three sections that make up the front are attached to one another.

3. Seen from behind you can see the fillet of glue that acts as reinforcement fro the joints.

4. The front and back sub-assemblies are then brought together.

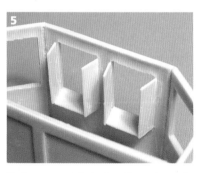

5. Counters and display boarding surround the front windows.

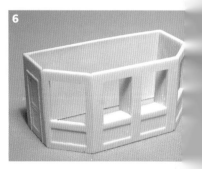

6. The main assembly is ready for the roof.

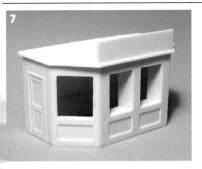

7. With the sign backing board already mounted, the roof is glued on top of the structure

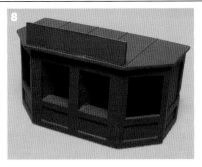

8. Red oxide car primer give paint a good base.

9. A streaky light tan colour makes a good first coat for a varnished timber finish.

10. This is followed by a streaky coat of chestnut paint ready for a third coat of varnish.

11. The completed news stand is now ready for the addition of papers, posters and fine detailing.

Goods shed

Moving up a notch on the complexity scale is this small goods shed that is very well suited to any minimum-space O gauge Great Western branch line.

With the construction of the main wall sections and the timber platform supports pretty much following the same processes as the smaller kits, there is very little more to add here.

Being larger, fixing the sides and ends in true right angles is arguably the most critical stage so, if you haven't already nipped out to your local model shop and bought an engineer's square now is perhaps the time to do so.

In common with other parts of this kit, the cast edges of the two roof slopes need a little fettling to tidy them up and to make sure that the joint fits together neatly when you get around to assembly. I found that by offering the two parts together while located on top of the walls it was easy to see whether or not the angles cast on the top edges of these parts would come together and make a good nice clean joint. Indeed, a good bit of careful filing and fitting was needed before the roof was ready to stick together.

Rather than trying to stick the whole of the ridge length (being quite long) together in one operation, it is a good idea to start by sticking one end first, let this dry, glue the middle section next and, once set, finish off by glueing the remaining end. I know this may seem a bit tedious and time consuming to do but it allows you to hold the parts together much more easily while the glue hardens and also lets you make slight adjustments to the alignment as you move gradually along the length of the ridge line.

While the roof is set aside and given time to fully harden, the wall assembly and the wooden supporting structure assembly can be brought together, checked for fit and, once you are happy that no further tweaking is necessary, glued together as the photo depicts.

As you can see, the lower framework juts out from the building on one side by just the right amount to take one of the four identical floor castings provided in the kit. Much as we have done elsewhere, check the fit, make any minor adjustments with a small file and stick the floor squarely in place on the supports and leave to dry for a while.

The quizzical amongst you might be wondering why we have another three floor sections left to use. Well, rather than provide individually cast floor part for the kits interior, the manufacturer supplies three floor sections as used for the external platform that can be cut down and fitted inside the shed. To do this you firstly have to remove the 'tongue' from the long edge of each part and then measure and mark the required internal dimension. Next, cut down the floor section using a razor saw so that it is slightly shorter than the platform fitted earlier. Each of the two outer flooring strips can then be glued in place such that they sit neatly in the rebate formed where the superstructure proper sits on top of the raised timber framework below. This now leaves the centre section which, as you can see, is somewhat narrower than the other two. Here you need to take the remaining floor casting and mark the exact width required by offering the oversized part into position between the outer floor sections in-situ. Then scribe a line on the underside using the point of a pair of compasses or something similar such that it is an easy task to trim away the excess resin with the razor saw as we did earlier. To ensure that the floor is fully fixed, simply spread a line of superglue along the long edges of the part immediately prior to inserting it into its slot, making sure that the upper edges are perfectly flush and level with the adjoining floor sections on either side.

As I wanted to be able to spray paint the roof separately, I decided not to stick it down onto the main assembly at this stage. If you want to brush paint your model you can fix the roof now but I would suggest that you do so after painting the interior first.

Before we can send the goods shed to the paint shop, there are a few more parts that still need to be added. The first of these is to glue the combined eaves/gutter detail to the tops of the two main sides. I used superglue to tack one end in place first and then, once it had chance to set, carefully ran more glue into the rest of joint making sure all was level as I did so.

1. The goods shed parts before assembly.

Moving on, we have the two sliding doors and door track assemblies to fix. The doors go on very simply indeed with a spot of superglue but the tracks above each door need to be positioned just in front of the hangers that, in real life, would support them. In order to space the track a realistic distance away from the walls, you do need to make up a couple of small spacer blocks from scrap resin material but otherwise this is a straightforward case of sticking with superglue.

With the model basically complete we can now turn our attention to painting. Having fibre-brushed the surface of the model to give the shiny resin surface a key, the easiest way to prime the shed is to spray it all over with aerosol car primer. With an intended livery of cream walls and a greyish roof it is logical to use white primer for the main part of the building and grey for the yet-to-be-fixed roof. Before going mad with the aerosol, it is perhaps prudent to test the paint on a part of the model such as the underside of the floor that will not be visible on the completed model, just in case it doesn't go quite to plan. I will readily admit that I have in the past found c brand of primer not to take particula well to the resin-based parts of so kits and yes, I had thoroughly shal the can for minutes on end too!

Happy that the primer has be given at least twenty-four hours to and harden, the other colours can r be applied. To speed up painting large area of cream walls, I decide spray matt enamel paints using Badger airbrush. Don't worry if haven't got one of these, you can as easily brush-paint the corruga walls without leaving too many br marks on the finished surface. W this is drying you can turn attention to the roof. To repre cheap and cheerful asbestos boarc a mixture of concrete, mid-br paint and a splash of thinners ca applied with a fair sized flat brush such that a streaky weath finish results. The timber platform staging is similarly painted wi greyish/brown mix and finally guttering and door tracks ca picked out, as in this case, with (Western chocolate colour to com the job.

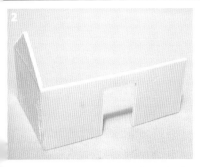

2. Firstly, one end and a main wall are glued together.

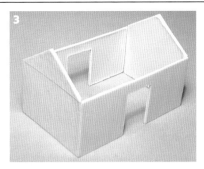

3. Two wall/end sub-assemblies are joined to form the main structure.

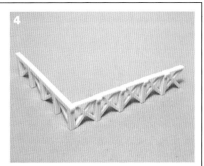

4. The timber support framework again starts with the fixing of a side and front.

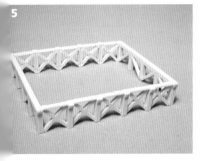

. All four parts that make up the support are ow fixed together.

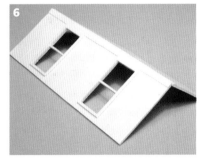

6. The two roof slopes are fitted and glued together.

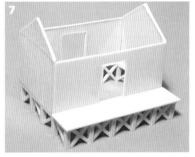

7. With the superstructure attached to the support framework, the platform is added.

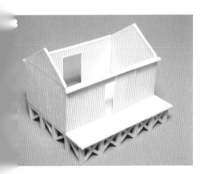

Next, rainwater gutters are glued in place der the eaves.

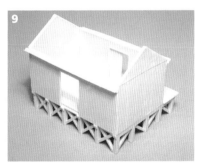

9. At the back there is no platform but note alignment of the wall and framework.

10. The internal floor is made up of three parts that have to be cut and fitted to size.

Close up of the metal rainwater pipes in tion on the walls.

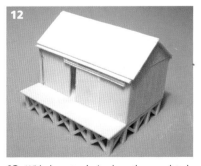

12. With doors tracks in place, the completed shed awaits decoration.

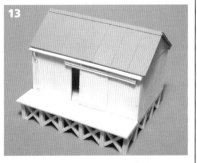

13. Primed with car primer, the shed is now ready for painting.

These terrace houses in New England, Peterborough, known locally as 'The Barracks', were built by the Great Northern Railway alongside its massive eng
shed complex.

Terraced houses weren't always plain; these examples were built on a much
grander scale.

These neat red brick examples face Oakham's Midland Railway station
Rutland.

A s the industrial revolution and the railways spread throughout Victorian Britain, cheap local accommodation was often needed to house the workforce for the new, very labour-intensive transport network and industry in general. Long rows or terraces of houses sharing dividing walls were laid out by planners, often right alongside the railways or the industries that they served. It is not surprising, therefore, that terraced houses have become a firm favourite with railway modellers and as such have over the years become the subject of many kits and ready-to-use models.

Metcalfe make this splendid representation of a brick terrace in card.

nby's Skaledale range contains left and right handed houses together with front and back garden walls.

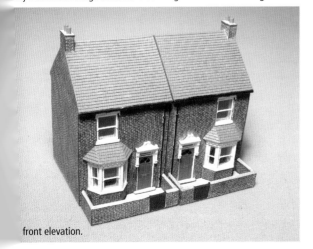

front elevation.

The rear elevation.

The completed cottage in a rural setting.

Unlike other kits made using the injection moulded plastic process, Will's Craftsman range of buildings do not come in a form that is ready to put together straight out of the box. Instead you get various standard 156mm x 76mm sheets of moulded bricks, stones, tiles or slates as appropriate to the model, together with preformed sprues containing plastic windows, chimneys, roof detailing pieces and rainwater goods.

To help and guide you through this halfway house to scratch-building, the manufacturer provides the modeller with full-size drawings of the subject building and a standard booklet detailing tips and hints on how this type of kit can be constructed.

The basic stages of assembly are :-

- Familiarisation with the instructions
- Marking out the plastic sheets
- Cutting out the pieces
- Adding windows, glazing and curtains
- Assembly of walls and roof
- Adding detailing pieces and rainwater goods
- Painting

The first task for the modeller to get cracking with is that of marking out the plain sheets of moulded stonework and roof slates. To do this you will need a steel rule, an engineer's square and something to mark the surface with. I used a felt-tipped pen so that it shows up in the photos but you can use a pencil or a scriber if you wish. Having placed the piece of wall sheeting stone face down, the first job is to measure and draw on the vertical lines using the square as a guide. So that you can easily set out the sheets, Wills provide you

with full-sized dimensioned drawings each of the parts together with sket elevations for you to follow. Ne measure and draw on the horizon lines before adding the door and wind openings in turn. Being face down, y do have to remember to draw out parts in the mirror image of the draw such that they are the right way arou when they are cut out and are seen fr the front (unless of course you wan build a handed version of the cotta Once you have marked the first sl out, double check that all of dimensions are correct and that openings are all in the correct plac appreciate this does sound like comr sense but it is well worth do particularly as you can't easily put of plastic stonework back once have been cut and trimmed to shap

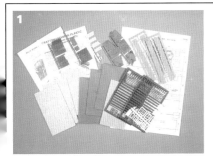

1. The building components

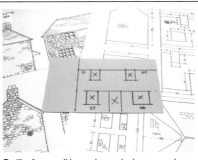

2. The front wall has to be marked out on a sheet of plastic using the scale drawings as a template

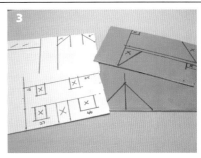

3. The remaining walls and roof sections are similarly marked out

4. To cut out a window you start by drilling a series of holes just inside the cut line

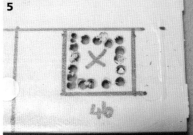

5. A window after drilling

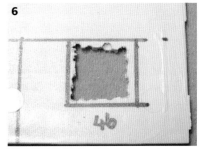

6. Next you cut through between the holes to remove the centre

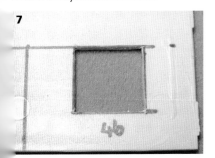

7. Finally the opening is trimmed or filed to its proper size

8. Windows that abut the edge of the sheet can be cut with a razor saw

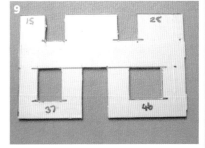

9. The cutting out of the front wall is completed

With one wall ready to cut out, you ould by now, be getting the hang of e process and the marking out the t of the walls, the chimneys and the f will all be easy to do in more or s the same manner.

Now for the cutting out! Being around thou thick, the Wills plastic sheets somewhat thicker than most other stic kit components and even most the frequently-used thicknesses of stic card for that matter. As a result ing is a little more difficult and ds special consideration before you mence work.

tarting with the easiest, the long ight cuts are best made on the flat, unfaced, side of the sheet using a sharp craft knife.

Being so thick, you do have to make several passes to cut right through. I find it best to make two or three passes along the cut line, first against a steel rule and then bend the two sides of the cut line back a little to open it up. This will reduce resistance on the blade such that another couple of passes will progress the cut right through.

As an alternative to the craft knife you can use a fine saw such as a razor saw or a small hacksaw. Both of these will do much the same job but remember, if you use one, to allow for the width of the blade along the waste side of the cut line.

Cutting out door and window openings that start from the edge of a sheet are easy to do. If you start by carefully saw-cutting the two sides of the opening, the remaining top edge can be cut using a craft knife. Windows that are completely surrounded by plastic are, however, another matter. To cut these out you first need to make starter holes through the plastic. If you are proficient with a coping saw, you could drill a hole at each corner of the opening and then saw between them. I, on the other hand, prefer to drill a lot of small holes so that I can completely remove the centre of the opening. By doing this, the final process of cutting to line is made much easier to do with just a

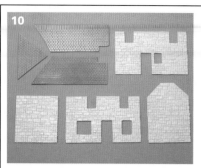

10. With the other parts cut out, the kit starts to take shape.

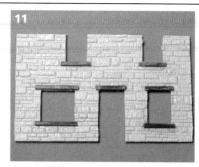

11. Sills and lintols can be added before assembly.

12. The injection-moulded window is fixed behind the opening.

13. Clear plastic glazing is next added.

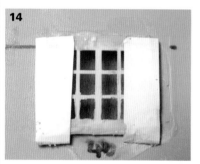

14. Paper curtains finish off the window.

15. The completed window from the front.

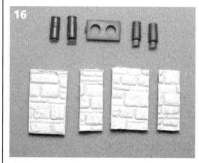

16. The chimney walls are cut out from sheet but the pots are moulded.

17. The chimney stack during assembly.

craft knife. Whichever way you choose to cut these sheets, always be prepared to tidy up the edges with a small file. A flat sided triangular needle file is, I find, the best for this purpose as it can both smooth the flat edges of an opening and get right into the corners without touching or affecting the two adjacent sides.

Once you have all of the parts cut and prepared for assembly and while the walls can still be laid flat, it is the best time to fix the windows, glazing and curtains. If you wish, you can at this point, also paint the reveals of the openings and the windows to prevent an otherwise awkward job later in the project. Being already moulded for you, the fixing of these present no problems at all.

As you can see, the rest of the assembly process and the order of construction now follows pretty closely to that of any normal plastic kit. There are a few slight differences that are worth highlighting here. Firstly, the butt jointed corners of the building are reinforced with specially moulded triangular section strengthening pieces that are glued into the rear of the joint. When these butt joints have been given sufficient time to set and harden thoroughly you will see a rather unsightly strip of plastic that really does need to be finished off prior to painting. In the case of this stone cottage, the corner first needs to be filed to remove any projecting bits of plastic before new joints between the stone courses are carefully cut and carved in using a craft knife.

With the rainwater pipes and gutters being easily fixed in place, the roof just needs its ridge and hips to be added. Here, as the strips of moulded plastic tiles have a flat bottom surface, you will need to file flat each of the intersections between the slopes, such that the ridge and hip tiles can be glued neatly on top of these angles.

Finally, in common with most of plastic kits, you just have to paint the model in the time-honoured tradition using matt enamel or acrylic paints.

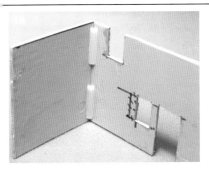

18. Wall joints are reinforced with special moulded parts.

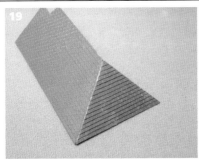

19. The first two roof sections are stuck together.

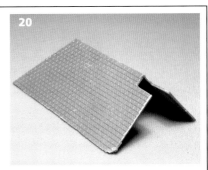

20. The third section is added.

21. A simple tab made from scrap plastic secures the chimney stack in place.

22. The butt jointed corner as it is glued together.

23. After filing and careful carving with a craft knife, the stonework is much improved.

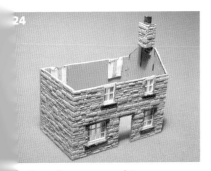

24. The walls are now complete.

25. The roof assembly is added to the walls.

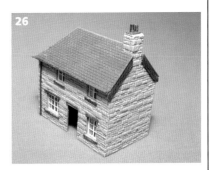

26. Verge boarding makes a tidy joint between the two sub-assemblies.

27. The eaves boarding and rainwater goods fixed in place.

28. The ridge and hips are filed flat to take the ridge and hip mouldings.

29. The ridge and hips in place - note the filler piece still has to be trimmed to size.

These corrugated Anderson shelters come with either brick or wooden ends.

As we begin to populate the layout which shops and houses, we often forget in our excitement to give a little thought to the yards and gardens that inevitably surround them. With brick privies a thing of the past, we aught to remember that most houses, even into the early 20th century, had outside loos, and curious little outhouses like these shouldn't be forgotten.

Even in more modern times we find a host of huts and sheds in our gardens and allotments. With a few nicely placed tools or accessories and with the addition of an odd figure or two, a simple shed, like the examples shown from Harburn Hobbies, can quickly make a lineside diorama come to life.

This is a common type of mono-pitched shed.

For shed spotters, this version has windows too!

typical plain double-pitched garden shed.

Small sheds for Vandal the dog.

brick hut could be used almost anywhere on the layout.

Harburn's small timber shed.

rger shed.

A mono-pitched version of the garden shed.

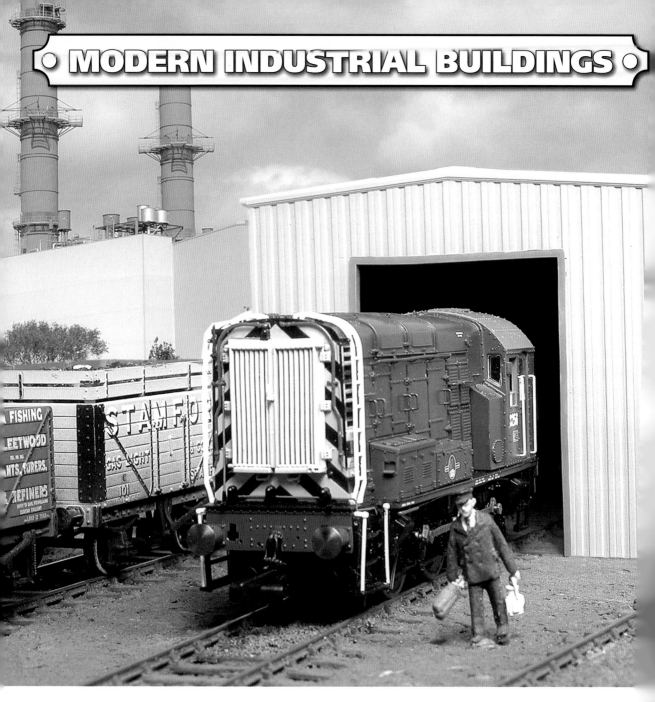

Industrial buildings have always played a huge part of our country's railway heritage, both sending and receiving goods and materials right back from their inception. It is no wonder, therefore, that there are many types of these available to the railway model maker in kit form.

For the modern image modeller the choice of prototype is endless. Not only does he have the range of modern portal framed structures like the ones featured here, but he can also employ much earlier building types left over from the steam age. Indeed, several disused steam sheds like the former Great Eastern Railway one at Peterborough's East Station site have at some point in time been turned over to industrial usage. Options, as they say, are infinite!

Having already reviewed the basics plastic kit construction earlier in book, it is well returning to topic to take a look at some of the m modern structures available to modeller. Large spanning portal-fra buildings have, for the last forty year so, become the industry standard building all kinds of factories, distribu depots, warehouses and for that ma

...vay buildings such as engine sheds
...maintenance facilities.

...rhaps the first choice for the
...ern image modeller are the wide
...e of kits in the Pikestuff range
...able from Modern Structures in
...ature in 2mm and 4mm scales
...ugh some of the continental
...es have suitable modern buildings
...To give the modeller an insight into

the basic assembly process we will look
at a straightforward twin-road engine
shed from Modern Structures in
Miniature/Pikestuff. There is a similar
twin road shed from Hornby but
we'll start with a simple engine shed
from Pikestuff's kit-basher range.

Modern Structures in Miniature Small Engine Shed

This small engine shed is ideal for the
odd shunter whether on a modern
branch line or industrial layout.
Described by Pikestuff as one of its
Kitbasher series of kits, this model can
be built up in a whole host of ways.

If you look carefully at the photos,
you will see that, not only do the sides
have a load of different window and
door positions marked by half thickness
rebates but they also have similar

rebates at various horizontal levels up
the buildings sides. This effectively
means that it is fairly easy to make the
kit up in three versions ranging from the
full height engine shed to two industrial
buildings with much lower eaves
heights. As you can see from the
illustrations, the kit comes with walls in
much smaller width sections than its
large stablemate such that it can be
modified much more readily by the
inventive modeller. Similarly, the roof is
in more sections and has a separate
ridge section that joins the roof slopes
together.

As with the larger models from the
same manufacturer, two or more kits
can be added together to make up into
quite complex structures with, if you
wish, varying heights for the differing
bays of your building. The possibilities
as they say, really are endless!

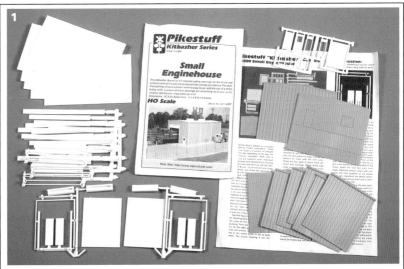

1. The unbuilt kit.

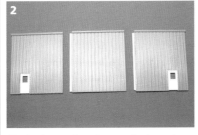

2. The three wall sections are fixed together
with jointing strips.

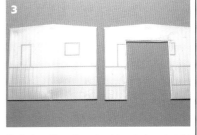

3. Each wall can be cut out to whatever height
and configuration you want.

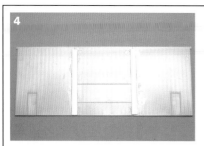

4. A completed wall section.

5. Assembly commences.

6. The walls are complete.

7. In this instance the ridge is a separate piece that holds the slopes together.

8. A typical roof joint as seen from inside the kit.

9. The completed model ready for painting.

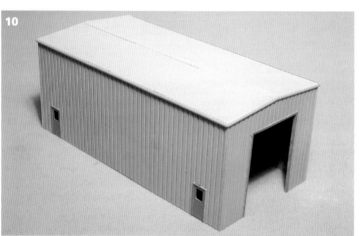

10. & 11. The engine shed has been given a coat of grey car primer and the doors have been picked out in matt enamel paints.

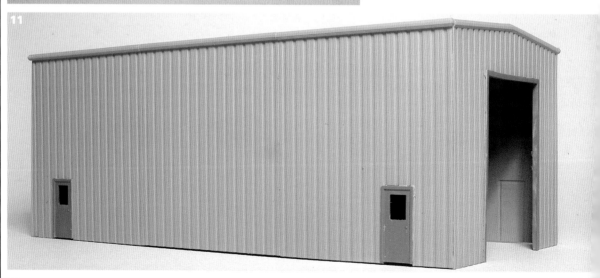

Hornby Engine Shed

Although very simple to assemble, this kit, which has recently been removed from Hornby's extensive catalogue, makes an interesting comparison with the Pikstuff model. This tin shed is an engine shed and comes with all of the openings ready-formed for you to get straight into the construction process. As you can see, this structure comes complete with brick walls around its base and has a wealth of roof detail that could easily be added to the Pikstuff model. The only thing that may need attention are the oversized up and over door mechanisms that are perhaps a bit gimmicky and could be easily removed if you so wish.

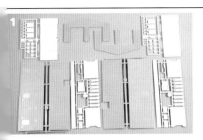
1. The Hornby kit displayed.

2. Construction commences.

3. These opening doors can soon be removed if desired.

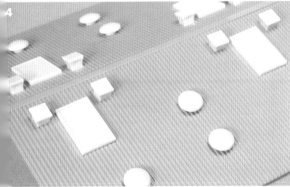

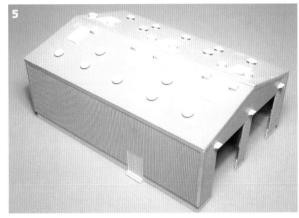

. A plethora of vents super-detail the roof.
. The building nears completion.

. The completed engine shed after painting.

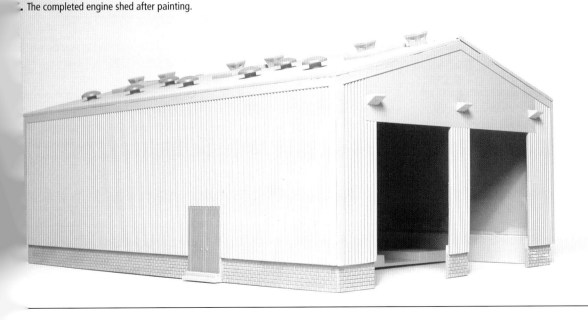

Modern Structures in Miniature Twin Road Engine Shed

This large engine shed is ideal for the modern image fan, having just enough room to accommodate two large locomotives. As the window and door positions are marked by half-thickness rebates in the back of each wall section, the modeller has the choice of making the kit up in a number of ways with as many, or as few, window and door apertures as he/she likes. Perhaps the obvious choice is to have two doors at each end or two at one end and one door at the other (like the one I built up), but by having one door at each end on one side only, the engine shed soon becomes a maintenance facility with room for offices and workshops along the side away from the track. If one

twin shed is not big enough for you don't worry, two or more kits can very easily be joined together to make very large and extensive structures indeed using the jointing pieces contained within the standard kit.

The same can be said if you want the kit to represent a lineside factory or warehouse, as an identical kit can be readily adapted to suit (although you might have to mark out the large roller doors if you want one in a long main wall section). As the ridge already divides the roof into two halves, another option for the more adventurous modeller is to make a neat vertical cut across one of the ends and you will have converted the standard kit into a low-relief model that can fit snugly against the backscene. These kits really are versatile and will, I am sure, end up made into many more

variants than the short list of possibili that I have just mentioned.

Construction is, as you can see fr the progression of photographs, re straightforward with no real problem all. The only thing to take care ove when you cut out the windows or d using the pre-formed rebates alre mentioned. Being quite thick, the pl needs to be cut through using sev strokes of a sharp modelling knife. will see that a couple of passes of knife will show through on the front of the wall without going all of the through it. I sometimes get to this s and turn over the part and carefull along this line from the front face us steel rule to guide the blade. advantage of this method is th prevents the possibility of an untid edge that can occur as the knife

1. The kit ready to build.

2. The first task is to select and cut out the apertures you require.

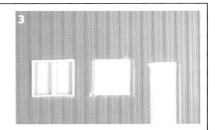

3. Windows and doors are fitted into the apertures.

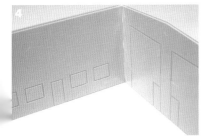

4. Assembly begins at one corner of the building.

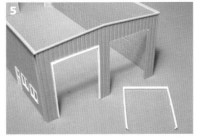

5. The main doors are trimmed with frames/flashings, doors are optional.

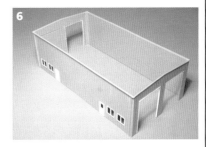

6. The two road engine shed takes shape.

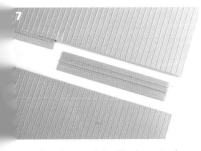

. Roof sections are joined by these simple grooved ridge pieces.

8. The roof element seen from below.

9. With the roof in place, the building is nearly complete.

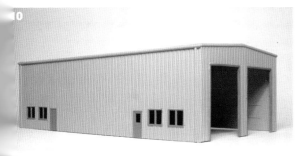

. A coat of grey spray car primer is an easy way to paint the kit.

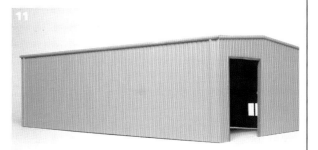

11. The same kit can be made up for general industrial use too.

ks through the plastic from behind. you wish, these buildings can be iled by the addition of ventilators roof plant and, if you want to increase the door height, say to allow overhead catenary to be fitted, you can always raise the kit off the baseboard by making prototypical brick plinth walls from strips of embossed brick plastic card five or six courses high, backed with two laminated layers of 40 thou plain plastic card.

Pitstone Windmill

Looking along the lineside, we find many interesting features that can readily be incorporated into a model railway setting. One such structure, the timber post mill, is the subject of an easy-to-make 4mm scale plastic kit from Dapol. On my way back from Railex at Stoke Mandeville, I came across this very similar twelve inches to the foot version at Pitstone, near Tring.

Dating back to 1627, Pitstone Mill is believed to be the oldest mill in the country. Despite suffering storm damage in 1902 it was restored and is now in the care of the National Trust who open it to the public on Sundays.

Close up detail.

Close up of the sails.

The base of the windmill.

Where the mill and mill base meet.

As you buy the kit.

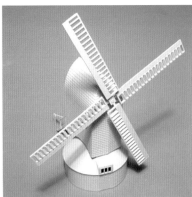

The completed Dapol kit.

The windmill's base.

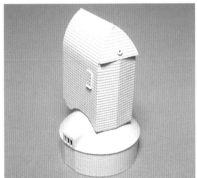

The top and bottom sections are brought together.

...ill from the rear elevation.

The steps up to the mill are added.

Perhaps not as well known to the layout builder as some of the other types of kit featured in this book are those made from an alloy of lead and tin, commonly known as whitemetal.

Due largely to size limitations of the production process, their cost to produce and to some extent the weight of the finished model (if used on a large scale), kits of this type tend to be limited to smaller structures such as shelters, huts and ancillary buildings. Indeed, well known manufacturers such as Roxey Mouldings, Mike's Models and Langley have all been making and selling kits of this type for many years. The guinea pig for our feature, Roxey Mouldings' Southern Railway platelayers' hut, although recently retooled, originally dates back as a kit to 1977!

The construction process is very similar to that employed when building resin kits and can be summarised as follows: -

- Familiarisation with parts and instructions

- Dry run of construction process prior to assembly
- Removal of any surplus 'flash' left by the casting process
- Assembly of the parts
- Priming and painting

Having already found out what to do and where things go, it is a very simple task to clean away any unwanted 'flash' from the casting process. In the case of this hut, which I must admit was very cleanly cast, I found hardly anything to do here at all; literally just the odd quick rub over with a flat needle file on a couple of the parts and I was ready to start assembly.

Here you have a choice of two methods. Firstly, you can put the kit together with a five-minute epoxy resin such as Araldite Rapid or alternatively low-melt solder the whole thing together. The decision is really one based on the individual modeller's experience and capabilities. If you haven't built a whitemetal kit before it is probably best to use glue and leave the solder to those who have experience.

Whichever way you chose, the ord of assembly is really easy to follow, an as you will see elsewhere, is pret much the same as we have used alread The stages are: -

- Fix end to one side and repeat wi the remaining end and side
- Fix both sub-assemblies together
- Fix roof on top of walls
- Add chimney and chimney cowl top of roof

The only things that you have remember about using epoxy glue to avoid putting and strings of wet g onto the exposed surface of your mo and to be patient and leave each jo to properly set and harden bef moving onto the next one. commonly find, when you h completed the assembly process, t you have a little excess glue show on the outside of the model wher squeezes out between the parts. D worry, all you have to do is to leave parts to dry and then carefully trim excess, now hardened, glue away u a sharp craft knife.

The advantages of low-melt soldering, I find, are that you don't have to wait for the glue to harden between stages and, with no stringy resin to apply, the whole process is a lot less messy. As I have already hinted at, you do need to be a little more experienced in the ways of soldering, particularly as an iron that is too hot can melt a whitemetal part in seconds and the whole kit could be ruined.

With this said, it is still well worth running through the basic principles for those readers who feel confident enough to give it a go. Firstly, and most importantly, you will need a low-temperature soldering iron (or a controlled-temperature one like mine), some low-melt solder and some dedicated low-melt flux. With these waiting in the wings, you firstly need to thoroughly clean up the surface of all of the metal areas that will become in contact with the solder by burnishing them with a fibreglass brush. Now comes the soldering. I start by brushing some flux on both edges of the joint and then bring them together so that they are held firmly in their final position ensuring as I do so that all angles are true and in perfect alignment. Next, a blob of low-melt solder is placed into the joint so that it tacks and holds the two parts together as it cools down. Having checked that everything is still in the right place, the rest of the soldered joint can be made by applying heat such that the low-melt solder just runs neatly into the remaining gap between the two parts. In some instances, I find it best to solder a short length of the joint first and then move along the joint in stages. Unlike ordinary solder, you do have to remember that if you apply too much heat the whole part will quickly become molten and the resulting bond will soon fall apart and you will have, unfortunately, to start the whole process over again.

Once you have built up the kit, all that is left to do is to scrub the surface under a running cold tap using some abrasive

1. The whitemetal kit.

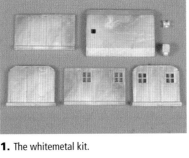

2. Parts are easily burnished using a fibreglass brush.

3. The first two walls are joined together using epoxy resin.

4. For comparison, the other two have been soldered together.

5. With all four walls together, the hut takes shape.

6. The roof fits on top like a lid.

7. A chimney and cowl complete assembly.

8. The completed platelayers' hut.

household cleaner on an old toothbrush to remove any flux residue. This process will also prepare the surface for painting which, once the kit has been left to dry,

involves a coat or two of standard aerosol car primer and a subsequent lick of enamel paint, much as we have used on other types of kit already featured.

To complement the terraced houses that we have already seen reviewed in these pages, many manufacturers - Townstreet, Metcalfe and Hornby included also produce a host of matching corner shops. With examples seemingly at the end of every terraced row, this popular building type has also become a must for many modellers. Here are just a few examples to hopefully inspire you.

Above: The most famous corner shop in the country is in Lister Avenue, Doncaster. This unassuming hairdressers was once home to Arkwright and Granville in 'Open All Hours'. Photo: Brian Sharpe.

Right: Andy's bike shop is a typical example of this building type where incidentally you can also buy second-hand model railway items.

Hornby's Skaledale corner shop in 4mm scale.

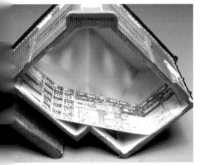

Left: The interior or the 4mm model.

Right: Hornby also produce the same corner shop in 2mm scale under the Lyddle End tag.

tcalfe's 4mm scale
d corner shop as seen
ore and after
struction.

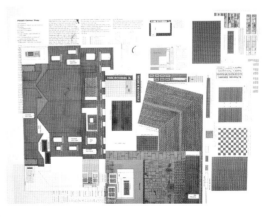

This simple shed makes a good introduction to building etched-brass kits.

Although a bit more expensive and much less common to find than some of the other alternatives of model building construction in the smaller scales, etched kits are well worth considering, particularly where, such as signal boxes and the like, you have a lot of fine detail in the windows and timber boarding that needs to be made from a strong but thin material. Most kits of this type are etched from brass or nickel silver and feature cut-out and ready-to-bend parts with half-etched fold lines. In some cases, etching is used as a structural basis for otherwise awkward structures; the D&S Great Northern footbridge is a good example of this.

To build an etched kit you pretty much need to follow the same basic processes. They are: -

- Removal of parts from the etched fret
- Cleaning up the parts and preparing or soldering
- Bending angles
- Soldering
- Laminating
- Cleaning off surplus solder
- Painting

Even though it is probably one of the smallest and, for that matter, simplest etched kits on the market that I have seen, we can still follow all of the basic stages as we build the ubiquitous garden shed in the Chatham Kits range, available from Roxey Mouldings.

Garden Shed

The first job as you will see from the hit list above is to free all of the components from the etched sheet. Simple, you might think. Well, yes to a point. The main consideration here is to release the parts (that are held in place on the sheet by tiny half-etched tabs) without bending or distorting them in so doing. I find one of the best methods is to cut through the tabs using a sharp craft knife or a miniature chisel while holding the sheet flat down on a scrap of MDF boarding. Sometimes, if the layout of the etching allows me, I snip the parts out using

some very sharp nail scissors that I usually use for scratch-building thatch cottages.

Having released the bits, you will see that the remains of the etching tabs are rough and look pretty untidy. To remedy this all you need to do is to take a small ,flat needle file and carefully file them away until they are flush with the rest of the part. To make sure that solder will adhere to the sheet metal, you will now need to clean up all surfaces using a fibreglass brush (the small refillable propelling ones from Expo tools are particularly useful for this purpose).

With everything nice and shiny we can now 'tin' the parts ready for assembly. Tinning is a process whereby a thin layer of solder is applied just along the edges of all joints such that, once brought together, solder will readily flow into the joint and hold everything in place. To do this, apply a little flux (I use good old fashioned Baker's Soldering Fluid) along the inside of the proposed joint and then wipe a thin layer over the flux using a reasonably hot soldering iron. Don't worry if the first pass doesn't fully cover the brass with solder. Just repeat a few times until the part has heated up sufficiently for the solder to take. Repeat this on the inside faces of all joints. Where you have to laminate two or more layers of brass together such as the door frame in this instance, just tin a slightly wider area on both parts such that solder covers the areas of metal that will be in contact, without any solder being exposed on the completed model when they eventually come together.

Before rushing into the main assembly process, it is worth noting that some parts are best attached while the etchings are still flat. In this case the door frame lamination can be sweated in place behind the door opening on the end wall. To do this, start by applying more flux to the pre-tinned frame and then locate it on the wall section that has been placed, back surface uppermost on a scrap of old wood. Now locate the frame so that the exposed edges when viewed on the outer

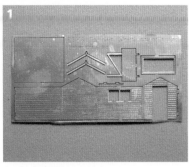

1. The etched kit as you buy it.
2. Having released the main walls from the

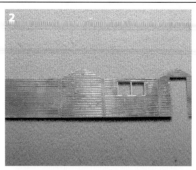

etch, you can clearly see how the model has been designed to fold up out of one piece.

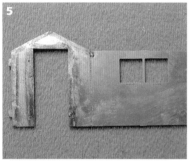

3. The roof is easily folded to shape along the half-etched line beneath the ridge.

4. Parts are prepared for soldering by burnishing with a propelling fibreglass brush.

5. Tinning will make the soldered joints much easier to do.

6. The door frame etching forms a laminated layer behind the door opening.

case of the shed, we only have two parts with simple folds to consider, namely the walls and roof. To ensure all bends are nice and crisp, it is best to form them against solid flat metal surfaces wherever possible (I often use the thick part of my engineer's square and a steel rule). Firstly take the part and line up the half-etched fold line so that it runs along and face the metal straight edge. Having checked that he alignment is OK, grip the part firmly against the metal former. Next take the second metal object, the rule in my case, and use it to spread the pressure on the 'loose' section of the etching as you bend the joint around the former below. In theory this will prevent distortion and should result in a much crisper joint than if you simple bent the part up between your fingers. Being an irregular angle, the roof needs to be folded to the exact angle such that it fits neatly on top of the wall. An easy way of checking this is to use one of the end walls as a template as you make the fold, offer it up inside the angle and make any fine adjustments so that it fits snugly in position. The wall folds the other hand should be at perfect right angles to one another. This is where the engineer's square comes in handy! quick check with this will soon reveal whether or not you have the angles just right. If not, the odd tweak and re-check will soon put matters right.

Now that we are ready to solder wall joint, brush both surface with liberal amount of flux and hold the seam together. Once again old block and bit of wood come in handy. In case you may find it easier to tack solder the joint with just a spot of solder inside the top corner of the joint first. Having checked its squareness and alignment, make a second tack at the bottom of the joint. Check again just to be on the safe side and if all is well make a third tack in the middle, finish the soldered joint, carefully between the tacks with solder, make sure as you do so that you don't apply too much heat such that the whole becomes unsoldered and falls apart.

side are evenly spread all around, and hold it in place with something that will not be affected by the soldering iron's heat (I used the tip of an old needle file or a wooden clothes peg). It really doesn't matter what you use so long as you can prevent the parts from slipping apart and, of course, you don't get burnt in the process. Next load the hot iron with solder and apply it to the joint around the frame. As it heats up you will soon notice the solder melting and, as it does so, runs into the joint. By moving the iron around the joint it will not take too long at all

before the whole lamination is hot. When you are happy that all is soldered, take the iron away and let it cool for a short while before you take the pressure off the tool, temporarily holding the joint together. If you haven't soldered before, the setting temperature is easy to spot, as the molten solder is very shiny but goes flat as it cools to a solid state. Once this happens, you can release the parts and the joint is complete.

Putting the soldering iron to one side for a moment, it is now time to fold up the parts that need to be bent to shape. In the

Before we look at the roof, a couple of detailing parts have to be added to the structure. Firstly, a small window sill needs to be soldered in place under the window. Location of this is very simple indeed as the part is 'tabbed' and fits perfectly into two small slots that have already been etched into the walls. Being very small, you will need to hold this sill in place using a small pair of pliers as you solder the joint from the inside of the assembly. The other job is to attach the door. To do this, the etched-brass bracing that will be exposed to view on an open door has to be tinned, folded back against the door's etched planking and then soldered in place before it can be fixed to the door frame. Once again, don't forget the flux to help the solder run and make sure that the door has been polished up with a fibre brush before you start. Using the small etched tabs that also act as dummy hinges, the door can be finally soldered in place on the main assembly. After all soldering jobs it is essential that you clean off any surplus flux or

soldering fluid due to its corrosive nature. To do this I thoroughly wash the parts under the cold tap, scrubbing the joint with abrasive household cleaner on an old toothbrush. Incidentally, the same process is very good at cleaning etched kits up ready for painting. Once rinsed and dried off, the parts can be given a final rub over with the fibreglass brush and the job is done.

To make up the roof, the two 'V' shaped verge boards (complete with etched finials) need to be soldered in place at each end of the main roof slopes that we have bent to shape earlier. Perhaps the best way to do this is to tin the back of the verge and place it solder side up on a scrap of old MDF. Offer the roof up to the verge and align the parts as far as possible. Tack-solder the apex and check all is in alignment (if it isn't, just release the joint with the hot soldering iron and start again). Once you are happy, finish the joint using the same overlapping tack-soldering method used for the wall joint. With both verges in

place, the complete roof assembly can be fitted to the rest of the building and, assuming a perfect fit, can be soldered in place from the inside of the building.

Having given the model a thorough cleaning up, the brass has to be primed before it can be painted. I usually spray brass kits with aerosol car primer largely as it makes a good base for most paints to adhere to and is relatively quick and easy to apply. The weathered timber of the completed shed was basically achieved by streaking brown enamel paint with a little grey whist still wet.

As you can see, the process of soldering an etched kit isn't really that difficult at all so long as you break things down in easily manageable stages. Unlike other types of kit, you do at least have the fall back option of being able to unsolder the joints and start again if they don't go strictly according to plan. The only real disadvantage to the novice is, if they haven't already got one, the modest additional initial outlay for a soldering iron, together with solder and flux.

With the walls folded to their final shape. joint where they abut is soldered together.

8. Verge boarding is added to either end of the roof.

9. A door and window sill add detail the model.

The roof is soldered in position and the ing is ready for painting.

11. Spray car primer is the next step. I think red oxide is the right colour for a 'shed'.

12. A quick coat of paint and a touch of weathering and the shed is complete.

The lower end of the lock and its gates.

urban scene. With many companie[s] including Langley, Harburn Hobbie[s] and Hornby producing canal boats an[d] accessories, modelling a waterway o[n] your layout is much easier than yo[u] may at first think.

Hornby produce a canal scene in both 4mm a[nd] 2mm scales. This lock and gates is from the 2n[m] scale Lyddle End range.

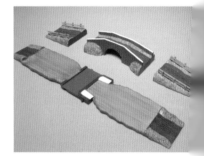

A complementary canal bridge, ramps and b[anks] are also available.

Although it is debatable whether or not canals and their associated structures can be classified as lineside buildings, I think they are worthy of inclusion in this book, largely as so many railways and canals follow similar routes and also as they are a very interesting part of the Industrial Revolution in their own right.

As the prototype pictures from Stoke Bruerne on the Grand Union Canal reveal, the modelling potential is endless with locks, canal workers' cottages, warehouses and even canal-side pubs to add interest to the rural or

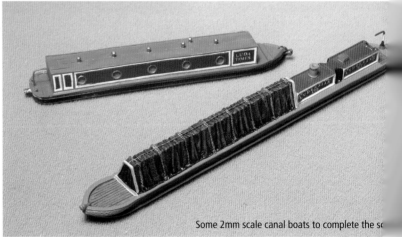

Some 2mm scale canal boats to complete the s[cene]

This large canal-side house is now a popular pub.

typical lock at Stoke Bruerne.

Partly scratch-built from plastic card and brass and partly built from a D&S etching, this Great Northern prototype is captured on the author's Paston Ridings layou

As we have already seen, the basic assembly processes needed to make an etched-brass kit are a lot easier and indeed a lot less daunting than many modellers may at first think. I have already mentioned in these pages that one of the significant advantages of etching is that very fine, complicated and ornate details can be successfully and accurately scaled down in model form. Despite a very fine outward appearance,

such structures, due to their composite layered-brass construction are in fact quite sturdy and robust.

There are kits on the market that use the intricacies of etched-brass construction for the more awkward, detailed parts of a building but leave the model maker free to use his/her own scratch-building skills to complete the remainder of the model. One such kit is the excellent GNR signal box superstructure etching from D&S

Models of Baldock in Hertfordsh This time saving product gives you that you need to make up the fi detailed upper section of the signal and allows you the freedom to m the remainder of the structure f whatever materials you might chose effect, this approach of hybrid kit scratch-building employs the bes both worlds and could, for m involve their first steps scratch-building.

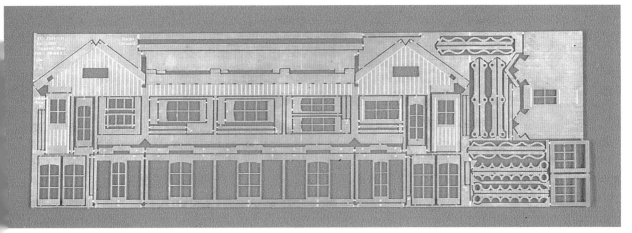

The D&S etching for the upper portion of a Great Northern Signal Box.

Based on prototypes found on the former Great Northern Railway lines from Hitchin to Cambridge and Peterborough, the kit itself contains an etched-brass fret for all the windows and doors on the three sides of the upper floor, together with a pair of etched windows and a door for the ground floor. As you can see from the accompanying photo, it comes complete with cast whitemetal sills, wall plates and finials. Although this leaves the brick or timber base, steps/handrails, balcony, walkway, roof and rainwater goods to scratch-build, I am sure you will agree this etch certainly takes away lot of work that would otherwise have be done.

Etched Superstructure

Once the D&S parts have been separated from their fret using a razor saw or a mini chisel on a hard surface, the builder must, for obvious reasons, decide firstly, which end he wants to fit the steps and balcony, and secondly, which of the alternative types of decorative bargeboard is preferred.

Having already introduced the basic tools and processes involved with this type of kit, you will see that assembly of this etching is a reasonably straightforward task involving the same filing, soldering and overlaying processes that we have seen while building up the much smaller etched

shed. Now I am sure by now some some of you have already noticed that the etching as bought makes up into a larger signal box than the one depicted. The reason for this is that I wanted a signal box slightly smaller than the standard kit, so I decided to adapt the kit and carefully removed the right hand end and set it to one side while I trimmed off the outer of the three bays to the front wall. Once this had been done and the etching had been filed up and prepared, the original end was then soldered back in place at right angles to the modified etching.

To achieve a realistic three-dimensional effect, each of the window frame assemblies has to be made up in turn and soldered to the fixed frames/walls, making sure of course that all of the glazing bars line up horizontally and vertically. Although this method of construction takes a little longer than a flat etch would, it does look a lot better and has the added advantage that the windows can be left in any position from open to closed that you chose. In order to locate the top inside the plastic base and allow the structure to be bolted together avoiding an awkward glued joint, I added three fixing plates to the assembly with each fitted with captive nuts. These were not supplied in the kit, but were very easy to make using scraps of spare brass from the etching.

Part assembled, the etched kit awaits detailing.

As part of the D&S kit, the sills, wall plates and finials are cast in whitemetal. Unlike brass, this much softer alloy is of a similar composition to ordinary solder and as such readily melts when it comes in contact with a hot soldering iron. To avoid this you can either stick these parts to the etchings using superglue or Araldite or solder them in place using special low-melt solder. Essentially, the process is the same one of cleaning and tinning parts before fixing them together as you would expect with ordinary solder but in this case, to enable the low melt solder to take to the brass, you will find it best to tin the brass with ordinary solder first, effectively converting its surface to whitemetal as you do so.

Now that we have completed the etched assembly, I am sure that you will agree, with a little added care and patience, there isn't really anything too difficult about the whole thing. With nothing to support the upper section it is now time to consider the base.

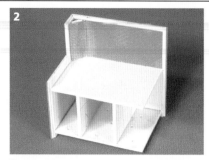

1. Base Construction Stage One – walls are made from two layers of 40 thou plastic card laminated together with an outer facing of embossed brick sheeting. Note the rebate for the etched window and the small holes drilled in the innermost layer of plastic which allows solvent to access and fully bond the adjoining layers.

2. Base Construction Stage Two – again using two layers of 40 thou plastic card bonded in the same way, floors and strengthening pieces are added to the structure. More embossed sheet is added to the exposed areas of the first floor and a chimney breast is added as on the prototype.

3. Base Construction Stage Three – the completed base with gauged voussoirs inlaid above the window and a length of old rail fixed in place as a lintel above the rodding aperture.

Base

Prototypically Great Northern signal boxes of this type were built with both brick and timber superstructures. Having in this instance, decided to build a brick base rather than a timber framed/timber clad one we first need to look at the three principal methods of construction open to use.

- Walls can be cut from thin plywood and be covered with brick paper or embossed plastic card. Although I have tried this pretty straightforward method in the past, I found some jobs like detailing around windows to be a bit untidy and the necessity for several types of adhesive to hold it all together was a bit of a nuisance.

- Walls can be made from 65 thou thick Wills brickwork sheets cut to size and stuck together. This is a quick and easy method ideally suited to this purpose. However, the inexperienced modeller should bear in mind these rather thick sheets are much harder to cut neatly than ordinary plastic card and the mitred joints that necessitate are a bit more time consuming to get right than other methods. In addition, any decorative brick features such as flush soldier courses and bands such as those forming brick lintels and arches above windows cannot be easily inlaid so that they are flush with the surface.

- The third, and my chosen method, is to construct what is effectively a laminated box comprising two 40 thou layers of plastic card faced with a 20 thou layer of Slater's embossed brick plastic card sheeting. Not only is this very easy to make but is also very strong and rigid into the bargain.

Whichever method you chose it is worth drawing your attention to the instructions which D&S provide with the etching and cast parts. Commendably, they include a scale drawing of the three main elevations and also help the model maker immensely with a three-dimensional sketch giving all of the principal dimensions for the base in 4mm scale.

Scratch-built Base Details

Using these notes and the part-built superstructure, the first job is to check the dimensions of the assembly so far against the drawings and make any adjustments to the dimensions that may be necessary prior to marking out the parts. As you can see from the accompanying sketch, it helps to work out at this stage just how you are going to make up the laminated walls. Doing this now will also enable you to compensate for the thickness of the layers and see exactly how they fit over each other at the corners.

Having roughly planned the way your model will be built you can now star setting it out on a sheet of embosse English bond brick plastic card. Unles limited by the length of the plast sheet, always try to plan whereve possible to get as many adjoini elevations next to each other. This n only makes things easier to mark o but also ensures continuity around th corners. The first embossed layer f the front elevation needs to be the f size of the wall and have correctly siz cut outs for the window and do apertures so, starting with a fresh she of plastic card, trim the long edge usi a sharp craft knife and a steel rule. T will ensure an accurate squa foundation for the whole setting-process. Then, with the aid of a sm engineer's square, pencil in the verti lines at the ends of all walls, mak sure that you keep the verticals lined with the embossed brick courses at same time. If you want to set y model into the scenery, draw a 10mm above and parallel to the bot edge of the plastic sheet. This ma will allow you to bring the scenery to the completed building when eventually fix it on the layout. Now the remaining outlines of all the w detailing window and door apert At this stage it is a good idea to do check the setting out with referenc the drawings and any photographs you might have, ensuring that all of the pencil lines are in the correct positions and that the doors and windows are where they should be. Once satisfied that all is well you can cut out the part using a sharp craft knife, steel rule and a cutting mat.

When cutting out windows and doors, I find it best to carefully remove the centre area of each window and door aperture leaving roughly 2 or 3mm to trim on the inner (waste) side of the marked opening. This is not strictly speaking essential but it does make the plastic easier to cut. Now take the knife and cut a line that bisects the point of each corner. Next, using the steel rule as a guide, remove one side of the aperture at a time, always cutting away from the corner as far as possible. This is where a new knife blade will reap dividends by leaving a clean, crisply cut edge. Repeat the process until all of the apertures have been cut out.

We now need to fully bond this layer to a sheet of 40thou plastic card using liquid polystyrene cement such as Mek-Pak, and set aside to fully harden. You don't need to bother about window cut outs in the backing at this stage, simply ensure that you have at least a small border all around the part. Now carefully cut out the window and trim the wall to size using the embossed layer as a template but making sure that you don't cut into the embossed plastic as you do so.

To stiffen the structure and to prevent warping, you need to add a second layer of 40 thou plastic card behind the first. In this case you need to make a cut out for the window (prior to fixing) that is slightly larger than actual size of the opening around the window. This will then form a rebate to take the etched window from the D&S kit. As you will see in the photographs, a series of small holes are then drilled through this layer prior to assembly to allow solvent to be introduced between the layers, permitting total lamination of the layers.

Once set, the inset brickwork to the

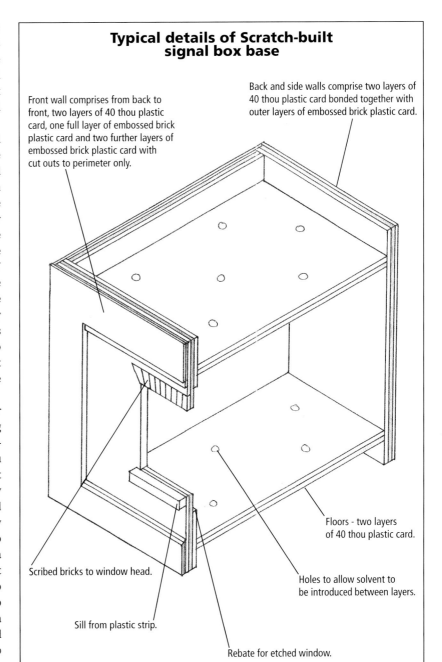

Typical details of Scratch-built signal box base

Front wall comprises from back to front, two layers of 40 thou plastic card, one full layer of embossed brick plastic card and two further layers of embossed brick plastic card with cut outs to perimeter only.

Back and side walls comprise two layers of 40 thou plastic card bonded together with outer layers of embossed brick plastic card.

Floors - two layers of 40 thou plastic card.

Scribed bricks to window head.

Holes to allow solvent to be introduced between layers.

Sill from plastic strip.

Rebate for etched window.

head of the window can be made. To start with, mark in pencil the area of the outer embossed layer above the window to be inlaid. Once happy, carefully cut around and remove the small piece of the embossed layer with a sharp knife and clean up the plastic of the underlying layer that is now exposed. Using a scraperboard marker tool, scribe the brick arch detail on a

piece of 20 thou plastic card and cut it out slightly larger than the corresponding area on the wall. Just like marquetry, trim the new segment down slither by slither until it just fits the gap perfectly. A spot of solvent is added to fix the inlay in place and, once dry, the bottom edge can be filed or trimmed flush with that of the underlying layer.

Having got the hang of the first wall,

The completed signal box interior.

the others are made in just the same way. Even the false floors and stiffening pieces follow suit, being similarly constructed but from two layers of 40 thou plastic bonded together. Although you can mitre the joints between walls, I rarely do. Instead, I butt joint the layers of 40 thou sheet together making allowance for the embossed layer at each corner. Being thin, the embossed bricks can be carried around the corners by scribing the plastic surface after it has had chance to fully dry. Once all of the parts have been made, the walls and floors can be assembled stage by stage much as you would do with a plastic kit until a rigid structure results. The only things left to do on the outside now are to add the window sill from plastic strip and make the feature brickwork that sits proud by a few thou or so. Having worked out that two picture frame-shaped pieces of embossed plastic, one with a marginally larger aperture than the other will do the job, it is relatively easy to mark and cut these out and stick them together first before aligning and finally sticking them in place on the model's front wall.

If you look closely at the photos, you will see that the brickwork is also exposed on the inside of the upper floor. This again is soon replicated by adding a second layer of embossed plastic card at the same time as you make a chimney breast from plastic card to fit diagonally across the inside of one of the back corners as shown.

I am sure you will agree, the whole process is really quite straightforward if you take your time, plan what you are going to do and split the process down into small, easy to handle stages. If you do make a mistake, simply make a new piece and try again. After all, only you will know that things didn't go quite according to plan in the first instance.

Interior

As you can easily see inside the signal box through the expanse of glazing on the upper floor, it is well worth considering some interior detailing before fitting the roof. Rather than spend a lot of time scratch-building all the internal fixtures and fittings, I decided to buy one of Springside's excellent signal box detailing kits. This, as you might expect, contains a whole collection of useful cast whitemetal bits

and pieces ranging from the frame and levers to the desks, block instruments, clock and even a notice board. If you can try to get permission for a visit to a preserved signal box you will soon get an idea of exactly what they contain. In this case I set things out pretty much as depicted by the drawings and photographs contained in *A Pictorial Record of LNER signalling*. The only real problem I encountered was that of how to fix the instrument shelf in the correct position above and to the rear of the levers so that all fixings are hidden from view above the ceiling level. After a couple of sketch designs, found the easiest way was to suspend the cut-down whitemetal shelf from the Springside kit by short lengths of brass wire. These were in turn soldered to a piece of brass section that was cut to neatly between the gable ends of the etched assembly.

Rainwater Goods

Although there are quite a few makes of guttering on the market, the signal box needs some prototypical half round section that can preferably be soldered directly on to the D&S assembly. Having found nothing totally suitable off the shelf, I discovered by experimentation that, with the help of a simple knocked up in the workshop, it was actually very quick and easy to make some myself.

To make the jig you first need strips of 1mm thick steel sheet that approximately 12mm wide. These then riveted or bolted to a 30mm wide base plate of similar material leaving gap between them some 2½ - 3 wide to take the brass rod. Don't worry too much about the workmanship, old scrap materials will do - completed tool will only be used few minutes for each length of gutter.

In reality, the most common width of guttering found on smaller structures are 100mm or 150mm, that's 4" and in old money, so you need to find length of approximately 2mm diameter brass tube. To make the gutter, secure the tube in the jig's central slot using a small 'G'-clamp and file away the top half of the tube. While filing, keep checking that the brass doesn't move or rotate and, after a few minutes, you will have a short length of half-round gutter section. Next undo the clamp and carefully move the tube along a bit ensuring that the two upper edges of the filed length are still flush with the two sides of the jig. Once you are happy that the tube is correctly aligned, reclamp it and repeat the process as many times as it takes to manufacture the desired length.

You will probably find that the newly formed gutter will require an amount of swarfe to be filed away and generally tidied up before you cut it to length with a razor saw. It is then a simple job to solder a couple of brass scraps to the ends and file them down to shape and add to some fixing brackets made out of fine brass wire where required.

For the rainwater pipes, which would prototypically be 3" or 4" in diameter, you need to cut lengths of 1mm diameter brass rod roughly to size. In the case of this signal box, the rod has to be bent twice to represent the offset projections that are located at the top of each pipe where it connects with the gutter before it can be finally trimmed to length. Small split pins can then be soldered at intervals along the pipe to represent the brackets commonly found on the cast iron originals. These are located to fit into holes drilled in the plastic walls of the base structure using a pin vice and small drills.

Roof

The roof on my model is very easy to make as it is simply covered by two sheets of Wills moulded plastic slates that are cut to size to fit exactly over the D&S upper assembly. Construction is pretty straightforward, although you do need to make a small aperture on the

back slope for the chimney stack, taking care that the outer edges align perfectly with the corners of the underlying brick walls. At the apex of the two slopes is the ridge. This can be made from two strips of plastic card glued on top of the slates with small lengths of 10 thou x 20 thou plastic strip added to represent the decorative raised joints found on the prototype.

The chimney stack itself is made from layers of Slater's embossed brick plastic card with a laminated core of 40 thou plastic card. As you can see from the cut-away drawing of a typical brick chimney, the whole thing is pretty solid and, once given time to harden, can be drilled to take the fixing peg of a suitable chimney pot. Unlike the ridge-mounting slot shown on the typical detail, the signal box's chimney is actually Araldited in place with a brass peg that locates directly into the top of the chimney breast on the underlying base section.

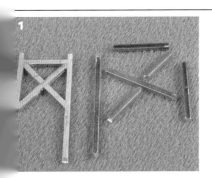

. The brass parts used to make up the illustrating are set out on the right alongside the completed unit.

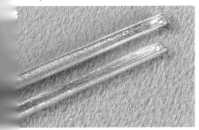

Completed gutters with stop ends attached.

Parts from the Springside signal box detailing are seen prior to incorporation. The instrument shelf is supported by four lengths of soldered to a length of scrap brass section.

2. Construction is progressing well as the D&S upper section and toilet are placed on top of the scratch-built base and balcony.

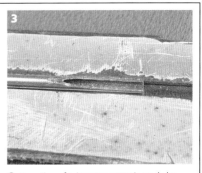

3. A section of rainwater gutter is made by filing a length of brass tube held in place on this simple jig.

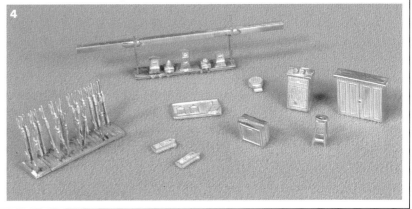

Typical brick chimney stack details

Hole for chimney pot.

40 thou plastic card filed to represent mortar bed.

Laminated core of 40 thou plastic card.

Strip of embossed brick plastic card one course wide.

Strip of embossed brick plastic card two courses wide.

Thickening made from an additional layer of embossed brick plastic card.

Stairs, Balustrading and Walkways

Although you can fabricate the balustrades and staircases from plastic section, I decided to make these parts from brass, largely as they would be a lot stronger and would be much less prone to damage whilst handling. With this in mind, we now need to take a look at some basic scratch-building from brass instead of plastic. Don't be put off having already seen the basics of etched brass kit assembly earlier in this book; scratch-building from the same material is in effect just the same process but you have to cut out the parts yourself.

Making a start, the balustrade and top newels comprise lengths of 1mm x 1mm square solid brass section that have been cut to length with a razor saw and cleaned up or shaped with a flat needle file. To help with soldering and assembly of the two panels required, I made another quick and easy jig this time from a scrap of MDF marked out with pencil lines using an engineer's square to mirror the exact layout of the components. The basic construction process is to firstly cut out the horizontal and vertical parts and solder one length of handrail square between two of the uprights or newels. Next cut one of the diagonal members roughly to length and file it to fit snugly in place. And then repeat the process for the other diagonal but with two small sections to making up the cross.

Having made a brass floor scribed with planking from brass strip and soldered it to the D&S supplied etched brass toilet assembly, the balustrade panels can now be added. To help hold everything in place while this takes place, I found it useful to leave one of the newels over length (this can soon be trimmed and filed to size once soldering is complete). The brass strip represents the timber framework to the underside of the balcony floor is added next together with stair handrails have been fabricated in much the same way. In order to save a lot of time and effort scratch-building a staircase,

Finally, to complete the roof and chimney detailing, small stepped strips of 10 thou plastic card can be cut to shape to represent the lead flashings that in real life seal the joint between bricks and slates.

moulded plastic stairs were purchased and were glued in place between the handrails.

Finally, the walkway is made up of two strips of 2mm wide brass strip soldered to brackets made from brass rod that has been flattened and bent to shape. The ends of these brass brackets are best left protruding on the inner face of the walkway so that they can locate and fix the completed assembly to the plastic walls.

Painting

Once the various assemblies were complete, I chose to spray the metalwork on my model with a couple of thin coats of aerosol car primer before spraying the main body with a cream mixed from a couple of the excellent railway colours from Precision/Phoenix Paints. In preparation for its final yellow brick finish, the walls and chimney stack were given a sprayed base coat of matt white before a mixture of cream, light tan and a touch of brown were brushed on top. Finally, the balustrades, stars and doors, etc., were picked out in dark brown enamels.

With all the elements of the model securely fixed in place on and around the lower walls, all that is left to do is to touch up any small areas of paintwork rubbed or knocked during assembly and mount it on a suitable base.

In conclusion, I appreciate that some modellers will find scratch-building too much trouble and effort to consider, when, as in this case, the hard part is done for you. I and many others find it really does add a new dimension to our hobby; not only does it give you much more freedom to chose almost any prototype that you want but it is really very personally rewarding into the bargain. If you have dismissed building something for yourself in the past, why not simply have a go? Find a small shed or hut to build and have a while. Who knows? - The bug might bite and you will end up with a new skill or interest!

Paston Ridings signal box painted and ready for fixing in place on the layout.

An end on view of Paston Ridings signal box with 'Parky' the signalman hard at work on the balcony.

WHERE DO WE GO TO FROM HERE?

Well, hopefully this book will have inspired and informed a few modellers to take the plunge and climb a rung or two up the modelling ladder.

For those who are just starting to build a layout for the first time, you should be able to get a few ideas of the kind of products that are out there to buy, and see how really easy most kits are to build. You will have seen how some modellers make the most of combining ready-made buildings and kits on a mix and match basis and may also get an idea for placing instant buildings on the layout temporarily until you have time to make a permanent or more appropriate replacement.

Having built up and photographed more kits that I care to remember in the making of this book, I hope the photographic progressions that have resulted will help you feel comfortable with various construction processes that you need to use. The only thing I can't do within in these pages, although I would like to, is to fully describe just what a feeling of fun it can be to build up a decent kit and to adequately convey that rewarding sense of achievement when you have just finished making up a model for yourself.

These, I'm afraid, you will have to experience for yourselves by having a go and building something up!

Those who at presently buy ready-to-use buildings may be inspired to pick up some tools and build up a kit. Even if you don't think that you have the time, inclination or experience, why not have a go? It really is a lot simpler than you may imagine.

Readers who already habitually build a certain type or make of kit may be tempted to broaden their horizons and have a dabble with another form. Indeed, some may wish to take their first few steps by scratch-building

Paston Ridings station building is built from plastic card and is actually based on the Great Northern Railway prototype at Wansford Road.

thatched post office is based on the ...otype at Alwalton, just a stone's throw ...y from the East of England Showground, ...enue for Warners' latest model railway ...avaganza, in October, 2008.

small structure. Don't think you have to build a massive mansion from the offset; that little brick shed at the back of a scene or diorama may actually be the best place to cut your scratch-building teeth. The main thing I find is that many modellers I speak to haven't got that initial half an ounce of confidence and self-belief to take the plunge and have a go. My answer is to buy some materials and mess around; it doesn't really matter if your first attempt is a bit shaky, I am sure you will soon get the hang of things. When I started to scratch-build, I found that I experimented and amused myself for hours using scraps until I was happy to put my newly found skills into practice.

I know that the wealth of tips and ideas relating to the basics of scratch-building cannot be written down in a couple of pages, and would indeed need another volume to

adequately cover them in detail, but I think it is worth including a couple of the buildings from my EM gauge Paston Ridings layout that might just inspire you to have a go. You may have seen some of the fantastic layouts featured in *British Railway Modelling* or its sister *Modern Railway Modelling* over the years and aspire to building something similar for yourself. You may, like me, want to have particular prototypes on your layout and, with no specific kit available, have no other alternative than to learn how to scratch-build. You may, like many other like-minded model railway enthusiasts, just want to scratch-build for the fun of it.

Whether you buy a model and plant it on the layout, whether you build up a few kits or whether you are ready to take the first steps in scratch-building always remember to do one very important thing – Have Fun!

LINESIDE BUILDINGS

Knightwing tanks, fillers and Portacabin.

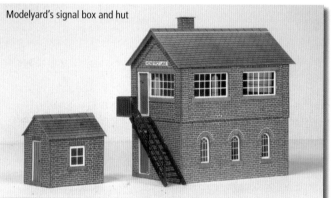
Modelyard's signal box and hut

PROTOTYPE INSPIRATION

Staverton on the South Devon Railway would make an ideal model.

USEFUL CONTACT DETAILS OF MODEL BUILDING MANUFACTURERS AND SUPPLIERS

Alphagraphix
23 Darris Road, Selly Park,
Birmingham B29 7QY
Tel: 0121 472 5252
Card building kits

D & S Models
46 The Street, Wallington, Baldock,
Hertfordshire SG7 6SW
Tel: 01763 288353
*Etched GNR signal box superstructure and
GNR footbridge*

Dapol Model Railways
Gledrid Industrial Park, Gledrid,
Shropshire LL14 5DG
Tel: 01691 774455 • Fax: 01691 778866
Email: sales@dapol.co.uk
Website: www.dapol.co.uk
*Plastic building kits – also available from
model shops*

Hornoplas
*Plastic building kits – available from
model shops*

Freestone Model Accessories
8 Newland Mill, Witney, Oxfordshire.
OX28 3HH
Tel:01933 775979 • Fax:01933 709578
Email: fma@fsbdial.co.uk
*Card building kits specialist – includes
Modelyard, Prototype, Bilteezi, Mainstreet
and other manufacturers*

Namodels
Graham Baker, 18 Lowe Tail,
Carpenter's Park, Watford. WD19 5DD
Tel: 0208 428 8773
Resin cast buildings and Accessories

Harburn Hobbies Ltd
67 Elm Row, Leith Walk, Edinburgh.
EH7 4AQ
Tel:0131 556 3233 • Fax: 0131 478 3233
Email: sales@harburnhobbies.co.uk

Hornby
Enterprise Road, Westwood Industrial
Estate, Margate, Kent CT9 4JX
Tel: 01843 233500
*Skaledale and Lyddle End pre-painted
resin buildings, Plastic building kits – also
available from model shops*

Kestrel Designs
Unit 12B, The Old School,
Station Road, Narbeth, Pembs. SA67 7DU
Tel: 01834 861427
*2mm Scale plastic building kits– also
available from model shops*

Knightwing
1 Wood Street, Huddersfield, West
Yorkshire HD1 1BT
Tel: 01484 537191
*Plastic building kits and accessories – also
available from model shops*

Langley Models
166 Three Bridges Road, Crawley,
Sussex. RH10 1LE
Tel:0870 0660416 • Fax: 0870 0660417
Website: www.langleymodels.co.uk

Peco
Beer, Seaton, Devon
*Plastic building kits – also available from
model shops*

Ratio
Ratio House, Mardle Way,
Buckfastleigh, Devon. TQ11 0NR
Tel: 01364 642764 • Fax: 01364 644466
*Plastic building kits – also available from
model shops*

Roxey Mouldings
58 Dudley Road, Walton-on-Thames,
Surrey KT12 2JU
Tel/Fax: 01932 245439
Email: dave@roxeymouldings.co.uk
Website: www.roxeymouldings.co.uk
*Cast whitemetal lineside huts, Chatham
Models etched kits and accessories*

S D Mouldings
96 Sparth Road, Clayton-Le-Moors,
Accrington, Lancs. BB5 5QD
Tel: 01254 238184

PEMS Butler Ltd.
The Red House, Culhays Lane,
Axminster, Devon. EX13 5SE
Tel: 01297 631435
*Pre-cut card building kits– also available
from model shops*

Skytrex Ltd
Unit 1A, Charnwood Business Park,
North Road, Loughborough,
Leicestershire. LE11 1LE
Tel: 01509 213789
*NMB Models range of 7mm scale resin
building kits*

Ten Commandments
100C High Street, Cowdenbeath, Fife.
KY4 9NF
Tel:01383 610820
Email: tencommandments @btinternet.
com
Website: www.cast-in-stone.co.uk
Cast plaster building kits

Townstreet
Greenhead Tower, Greenhead Gill,
Grasmere, Cumbria. LA22 9RW
Tel:01539 435465 (Mail Order only)
Cast plaster building kits

The Thank You Bit

Before the book is complete, just like a speech at the Oscars, there are a few people who I would like to thank for their help in the making of this book. Firstly, as Head of Production and Design, the bubbly Jayne Thorpe and her sidekick Ryan have done a smashing job putting my pictures and words together; *BRM's* Managing Editor, David Brown for his words of advice (OK, so it was mainly sitting around discussing mostly unrelated things in pubs!); Warner's jovial Publisher, John Greenwood for letting me loose with this project and for getting this book on the streets; Warner's Chairman and old friend, Michael Warner for his kind words of encouragement and support, and finally, 'the boss', for her tolerance with me and all of the mess and clutter that I generate while I am in full modelling mode.